365
EXERCISES
for the MIND

Pierre Berloquin

Sterling Publishing Co., Inc.
New York

I wish to thank Kathryn Bernard, who has played an essential role in bringing this book to life and has put her puzzling talent into most of the material.

Book design by Pierre Berloquin

10 9 8 7 6 5 4 3

This edition published by Sterling Publishing Co., Inc.
387 Park Avenue South, New York, NY 10016
Previously published by Barnes & Noble, Inc.,
by arrangement with Pierre Berloquin.
© 1998 by Pierre Berloquin
Distributed in Canada by Sterling Publishing
C/o Canadian Manda Group, 165 Dufferin Street
Toronto, Ontario, Canada M6K 3H6

Sterling ISBN 1-4027-2469-1

For information about custom editions, special sales, premium and corporate purchases, please contact Sterling Special Sales Department at 800-805-5489 or specialsales@sterlingpub.com.

Introduction

To solve or not to solve: Do we have a choice, really? Solving puzzles is the last and only redeeming activity a lively mind can engage in. Other rewarding occupations are gradually being taken over by machines and computers. We are deprived of all obvious logical business. Nothing is left to our restless minds but puzzling, puzzling, puzzling.

Today, puzzledom is our last proving ground. It opens a path to a virtual jungle that needs no modem, no cosmic network, no extravagantly electronic construction—only a run-of-the-mill piece of paper covered with traditional, apparently understandable, lines and signs. Yes, *apparently* understandable: this is where the line is drawn between the calm waters of reading and the perilous straits of the brain twister. In the quicksand of mental booby traps, expect no sure step, doubt every certainty—however tempting. Within the no-holds-barred space of a puzzle, keep your back to the wall . . . if you can find one.

Besides, puzzle trekking is a sure cure to all present world anxieties, an evident preparation for any surprise or shock of the future. Practice these exercises. Make my personal motto yours as well:

A puzzle a day keeps the hassle away.

–Pierre Berloquin
1998

Key to the Puzzle Icons

The icon at the upper left-hand corner of each puzzle indicates the particular skill being exercised and the puzzle's level of difficulty.

Here is the key to those icons:

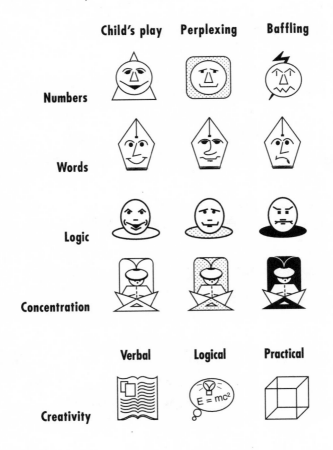

PUZZLES

Solutions begin on page 367.

If all the diagonals were removed, how many squares and rectangles would there be in this figure?

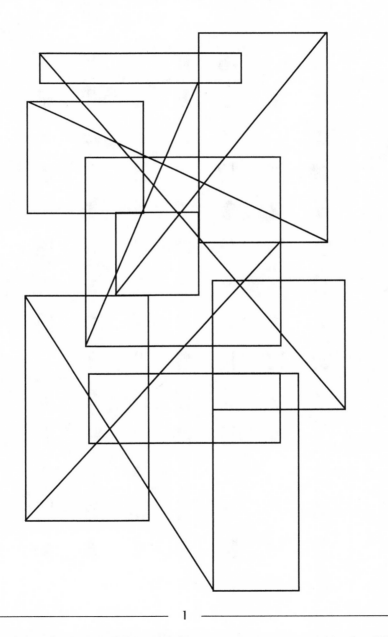

What is the logical relationship or pattern of the light-face numbers below? Which boldface number fits into this relationship (and thus should be lightface)?

1	15	**16**	**17**	18	9	**8**
7	**2**	6	**5**	**4**	3	**17**
16	15	3	12	**11**	**10**	9
10	**11**	12	**4**	3	**2**	**1**
9	**8**	**7**	6	**5**	**7**	9
11	**13**	15	**17**	9	6	18
17	3	9	**2**	**8**	**8**	**7**
2	**4**	6	**8**	**10**	**8**	12
14	**16**	18	**17**	9	**7**	**5**
3	**1**	**8**	**10**	**15**	**2**	**4**
6	**8**	**11**	**10**	12	**10**	**1**
3	12	**5**	12	**4**	**7**	9
13	6	**8**	**4**	**13**	**11**	15
11	**14**	**13**	**1**	**5**	**4**	**1**

Find seven different tools beginning with at least two of these letters.

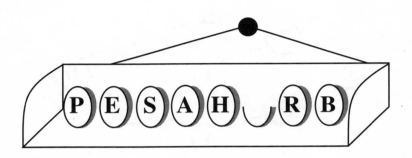

Add contiguous numbers (horizontally and vertically) so that they total 45. Each number may be used only once.

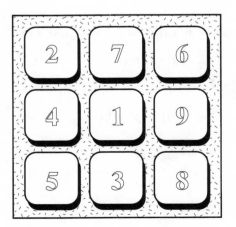

How many times can you read 0707? The sequence is valid only if the numbers are joined by a line.

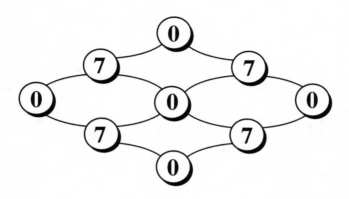

If this text were arranged alphabetically, what would the 13th word be?

Bouillabaisse is only good because cooked by the French, who, if they cared to try, could produce an excellent and nutritious substitute out of cigar stumps and empty matchboxes.

Norman Douglas

Fill in the blanks. Each side of the square is a logical sequence. The arrows indicate a common number.

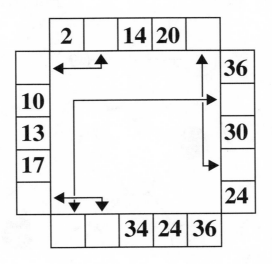

Find seven different ways to make pairs with these numbers.

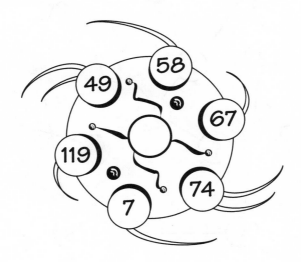

Find eleven multiples of 3 on this grid. Each multiple is composed of a series of digits joined by line segments (or just one digit). Each digit may be used only once.

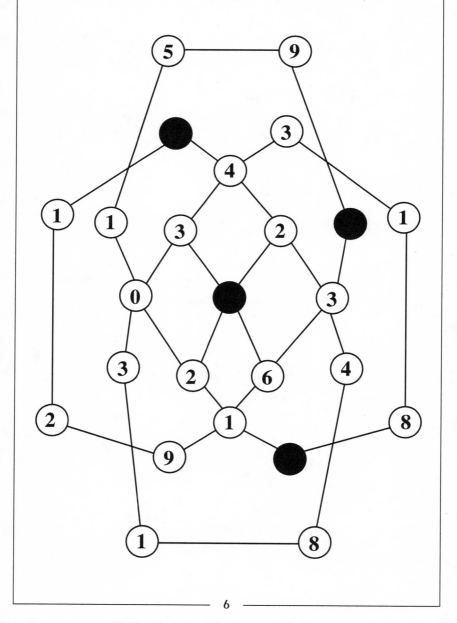

Use the first quote from Francis Bacon to find the second from William Congreve. The numbers under each letter in the second sentence show which word they come from in the first.

THERE   IS   IN   HUMAN   NATURE   GENERALLY
  1   2   3   4   5   6

MORE   OF   THE   FOOL   THAN   OF   THE   WISE.
  7   8   9   10   11   12   13   14

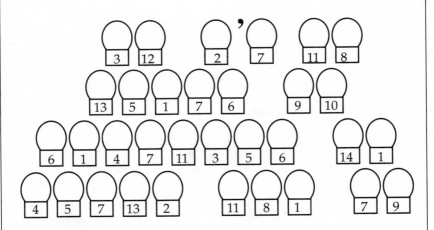

Can you find seven shorter words that compose the long one below? For example, *intergenerational* is made up of *in*, *gene*, *ratio*, *era*, *ration*, etc.

...industrialization...

What is the missing number?

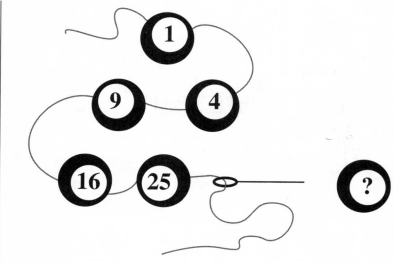

If the squares were circles, the circles were triangles, and the triangles were squares, how many

circles would intersect a triangle?
squares would be within a circle?
triangles would enclose a square?

Fill in the blanks. The arrows indicate a common letter.

Open or shut ....

Wanders ....

Paper file ....

Spotted ....

Connect these ten numbers. Each number may be used only once and must have no divisor in common with the following one. Connecting lines may cross over each other.

111   35   32

49   19   28   51

22   18   85

Using the listed items, devise a system that will logically determine the missing price.

Fish

Trout 20

Salmon 19

Plaice 16

Mackerel .... ?

Find seven different ways to make pairs with these words. (For example, *cow*, *calf*, *kid*, *cat*: *cow* and *calf* are the same species; *calf* and *kid* are the young of the species, *cat* and *calf* have the same first two letters.)

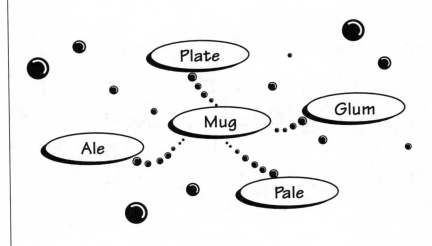

Plate

Mug

Glum

Ale

Pale

Fill in the blanks to find an Anthony Hope quotation. The letters of the quotation are in alphabetical order in each column of the lower figure. Going from left to right, pick a letter from each column in the lower figure to compose the quote. Skip a column when figuring a space between words, and use each letter from each column once. Some lines of the quote break in the middle of words.

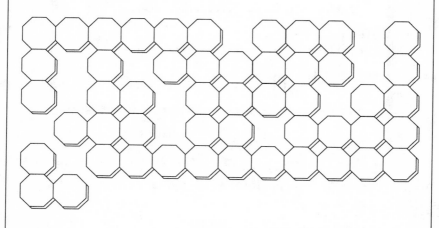

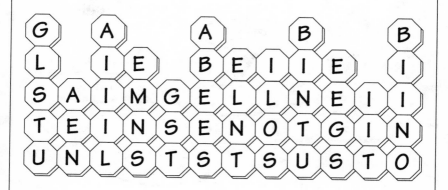

Complete this magic square so that it contains all of the numbers from 1 to 25. The sum of each line, column, and each of the two diagonals should be 65.

1		22			65
7		3	11		65
13	21		17	5	65
19	2		23		65
25		16			65

65   65

65   65   65   65   65

Which of these alcoholic drinks is distinct from the others?

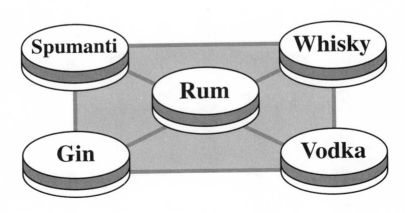

Use a series of lines to join contiguous numbers whose sum equals 75. Start at "a" and finish at "b."

a

1	2	3	5	5	6	7
5	6	4	1	3	5	7
3	2	5	4	9	4	2
5	4	9	6	2	8	5
2	3	1	8	3	4	5
5	2	8	2	3	4	9
4	6	3	8	1	4	5
7	1	2	1	4	2	5
4	3	5	8	1	5	2
8	6	1	4	1	2	4
2	8	4	6	2	5	7
2	4	8	5	1	1	2
4	6	5	2	3	8	4
2	5	5	2	2	4	1

b

SURFING

During summer vacation, four children — including Alex, Belinda, and Eric — spend their days at the beach. One day at lunch their mother asks: "Did anyone go surfing this morning?"

The oldest child answers:

> I wasn't paying very close attention to the others, but I think Alex and Belinda weren't together.

> However, if Alex did go surfing, it wasn't alone.

> If Eric surfed, Alex and Belinda were with him.

Who went surfing?

Find the signs (+,−) that complete the equations.

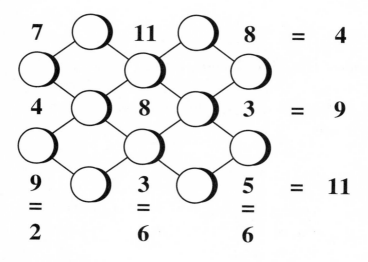

7 ◯ 11 ◯ 8 = 4

4 ◯ 8 ◯ 3 = 9

9 ◯ 3 ◯ 5 = 11
=   =   =
2   6   6

If the first square were turned upside down and placed on top of the second, you would be able to read the beginning of a sentence. After you have determined what that part of the sentence says, complete the problem it contains.

Words from a Jane Austen quote are scattered in the frame below. Following the arrows and using each word once, fill in the blanks to reveal the quote.

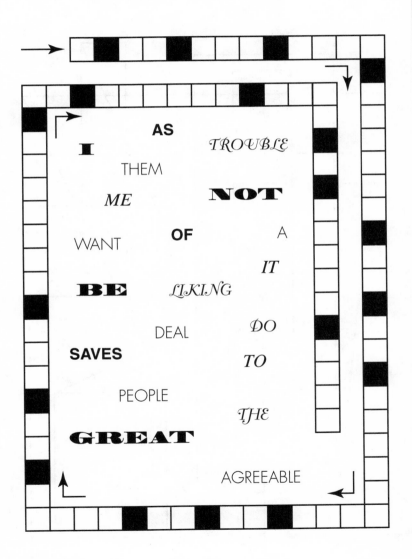

I   AS   *TROUBLE*

THEM

ME   **NOT**

WANT   **OF**   A

IT

BE   *LIKING*

DEAL   *DO*

SAVES   *TO*

PEOPLE

THE

GREAT

AGREEABLE

If all the diagonals were removed, how many squares and rectangles would there be in this figure?

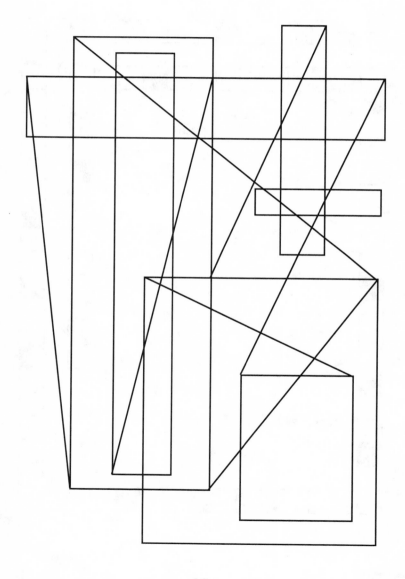

Replace each dot below with either 1, 2, 4, 5, or 6 to make the problem add up correctly. Each number may be used only once.

$$
\begin{array}{r}
5\ .\ .\ . \\
+\ 8\ 7\ 4\ 3 \\
\hline
1\ .\ 3\ 5\ . \\
\end{array}
$$

Fill in the blanks above the clue in italics. Then fill in the blanks of the frame, using those same letters. The 2-headed arrows indicate a common letter.

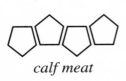

calf meat

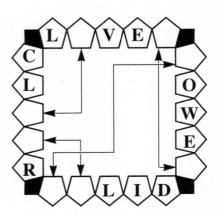

Make seven longer words from *can* by adding letters to it. For example, by adding letters to *hat*, you can get *t*hat, hat**e**, **c**hat**ty**, **s**hat**ter**, hat**less**, hat**ch**, etc.

...**can**...

Fill in the blanks. Each line is a logical sequence. The arrows indicate a common number.

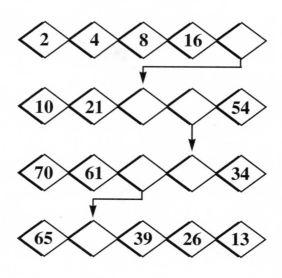

Insert +, −, and/or parentheses between the numbers to find the total.

$$=$$

$$\boxed{45}$$

Connect these twelve colors. Each color may be used only once and no two consecutive colors may have any letters in common. Connecting lines may cross over each other.

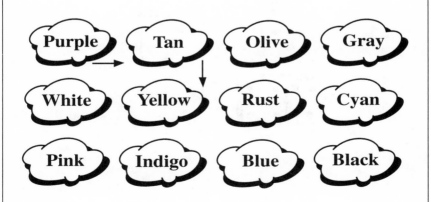

What is the numerical relationship of the dominoes below? Which domino is missing? (Their physical arrangement is not important.)

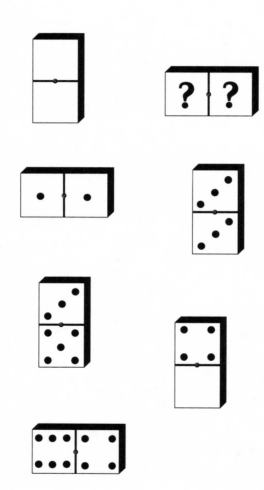

Both grids contain the same words, spelled horizontally or vertically. If a word is spelled forward in one grid, it is spelled backward in the other. Find all the words.

M	S	A	L	C	A		B	K	P	A	S	T	A	E
A	K	R	A	N	S		O	N	O	K	T	S	R	T
C	C	B	N	I	S		N	A	W	O	O	E	S	E
H	A	A	E	L	E		D	L	D	O	C	L	E	H
E	R	L	S	E	M		F	E	Z	K	A	N	C
T	R	E	R	V	B	I	R	A	A	B	A	A
E	A	S	A	A	L	I	T	B	D	R	L	M
E	B	T	I	J	Y	E	X	A	T	E	A	R	V
N	O	I	L	L	A	T	A	B	A	X	E	D	Z
E	A	G	L	E		E	L	G	A	E
N	B	A	S	E	B	A	T	A	L	L	I	O	N
W	X	R	S	T	E	S	A	B	E	Y	B	O	C
O	E	E	T	B	I	T	B	L	L	A	J	R
B	D	V	O	A	R	I	R	L	B	R	A	O
S	A	E	C	Z	E	F	I	I	M	R	V	S
S	G	I	K	O	D	L	D	G	E	E	A	E	S
O	I	L	A	O	W	A	N	A	V	S	C	L	B
R	R	L	D	K	O	N	O	D	E	S	K	I	O
C	B	E	E	A	P	K	B	E	R	A	S	N	W

These numbers have many properties in common but do not share all the same traits. Find seven different reasons for determining what makes one or more of these numbers distinct from the rest.

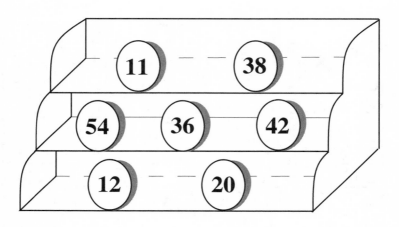

Make a word from the letters below, using each letter at least once. One letter must connect to another by a line in the diagram.

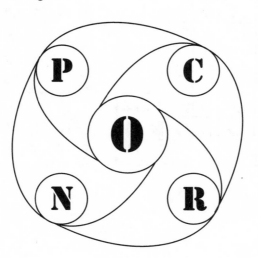

What is the logical relationship or pattern of the light-face numbers below? Which boldface number fits into this relationship (and thus should be lightface)?

1	**2**	**3**	4	**5**	**6**	7
8	**9**	10	**11**	**12**	13	**14**
15	**16**	**17**	18	**19**	**20**	**21**
22	23	**24**	25	**26**	**27**	28
29	**30**	**31**	**32**	33	34	**35**
36	**37**	38	**39**	**40**	**41**	**42**
43	44	**45**	46	**47**	**48**	49
50	**51**	**52**	**53**	54	55	**56**
57	**58**	59	**60**	**61**	**62**	**63**
64	65	**66**	**67**	**68**	**69**	70
71	**72**	**73**	**74**	75	76	**77**
78	**79**	80	**81**	**82**	**83**	**84**
85	86	**87**	**88**	89	**90**	91
92	93	**94**	**95**	96	**97**	**98**

Follow the arrows as you fill in the blanks. Sum totals at arrows' ends must add up.

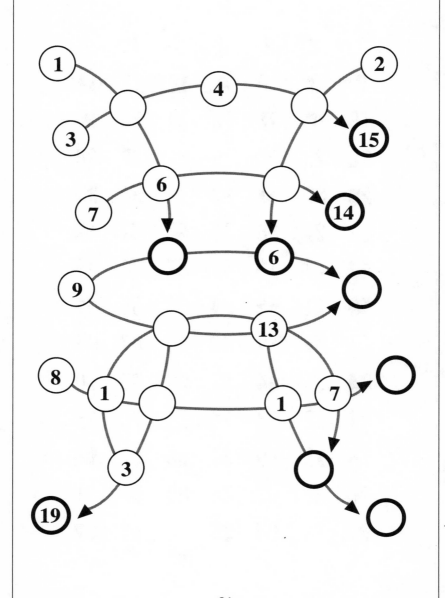

These words and what they represent have many properties in common but do not share all the same traits. Find seven different reasons for determining what makes one or more of these words distinct from the rest.

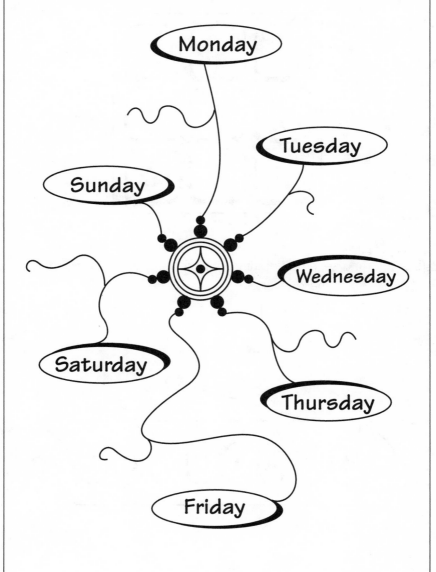

Add contiguous numbers (horizontally and vertically) so that they total 25. Each number may be used only once.

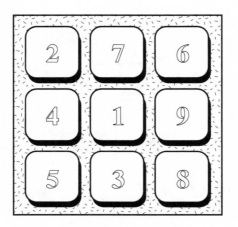

Find seven different fruits beginning with at least two of these letters.

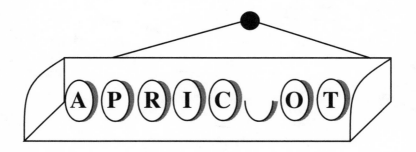

If this text were arranged alphabetically, what would the 13th word be?

The megalomaniac differs from the narcissist by the fact that he wishes to be powerful rather than charming, and seeks to be feared rather than loved. To this type belong many lunatics and most of the great men of history.

Bertrand Russell

How many times can you read 123? The sequence is valid only if the numbers are joined by a line.

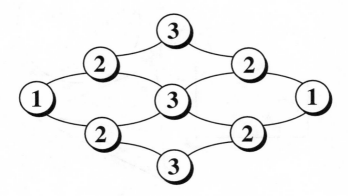

If the squares were circles, the circles were triangles, and the triangles were squares, how many

[ ] circles would intersect a triangle?

[ ] squares would be within a circle?

[ ] triangles would enclose a square?

Complete the equation by filling in the five omissions with 1, 2, 3, 5, and 6. Each number may be used only once.

$$(... + ... - ...) \times ... \div ... = 4$$

Find nine synonyms of SKILLFUL. Each word is written with horizontally and/or vertically connected letters. Each letter may be used only once.

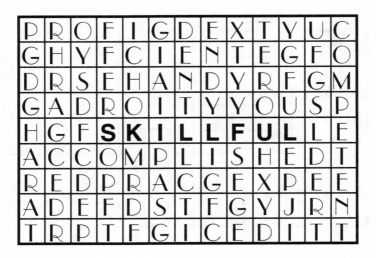

P	R	O	F	I	G	D	E	X	T	Y	U	C
G	H	Y	F	C	I	E	N	T	E	G	F	O
D	R	S	E	H	A	N	D	Y	R	R	G	M
G	A	D	R	O	I	T	Y	Y	O	U	S	P
H	G	F	**S**	**K**	**I**	**L**	**L**	**F**	**U**	**L**	L	E
A	C	C	O	M	P	L	I	S	H	E	D	T
R	E	D	P	R	A	C	G	E	X	P	E	E
A	D	E	F	D	S	T	F	G	Y	J	R	N
T	R	P	T	F	G	I	C	E	D	I	T	T

Make seven different sentences using only the words in this quote from George Bernard Shaw.

*The fickleness of the women
I love is only equalled by the
infernal constancy of the women
who love me.*

The figure on the left has ten currencies spelled forward or backward, in horizontally and/or vertically connected squares, but the figure on the right has only nine of these same currencies. Find all the currencies and identify the one missing on the right.

A	M	Y	N	N	E	P	I	D	F		N	A	R	F
R	Z	L	O	T	Y	M	R	C	R		C	M	A	R
K	A	L	L	O	D	A	H	N	A		N	E	P	K
O	R	K	R	O	L	F					N	C	O	P
O	P	R	I			D	N	U	Y		L	L	Z	
U	T	O	N	N	O	L	F	P	O	R	A	K	L	
N	A	N	A	I	R	T	A	C	U	D	O	R	O	
D	C	U	D	M	A	H	R	I	D	A	N	Y	T	

If the hexagons were placed one on top of another, what picture would you be able to see?

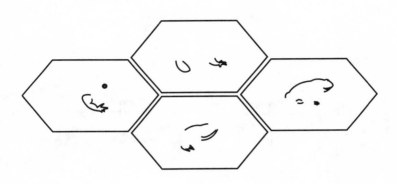

Most of the letters in this square are part of a logical pattern. However, one or more letters deviate from this pattern. Find the mistake.

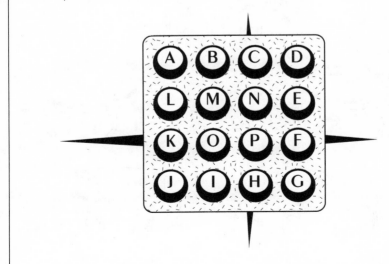

The arrows show the first two crabs in a sequence that is determined by some physical attribute(s) of the crabs. Provide the reasoning that allows the rest of the crabs to be joined in this sequence. Then give the full sequence by number. (In some cases, there may be more than one sequence that satisfies the pattern.)

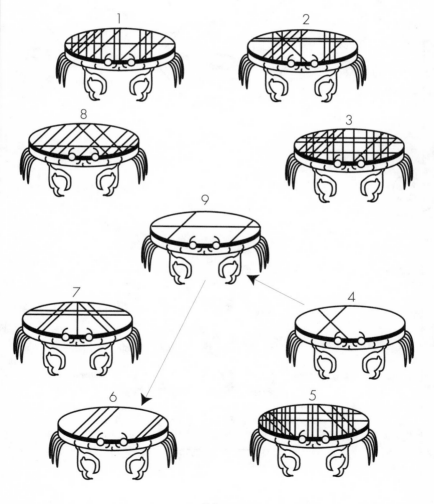

Insert +, −, x, and/or parentheses between the numbers to find the total.

1 2 3 4 5 6 7 8 9

=

46

Connect these twelve items of clothing. Each item may be used only once and no two consecutive items may have any letters in common. Connecting lines may cross over each other.

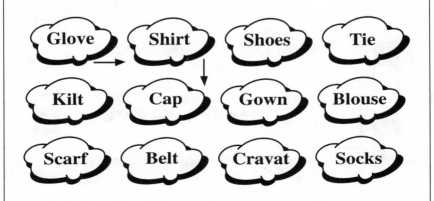

Words from a T. S. Eliot quote are scattered in the frame below. Following the arrows and using each word once, fill in the blanks to reveal the quote.

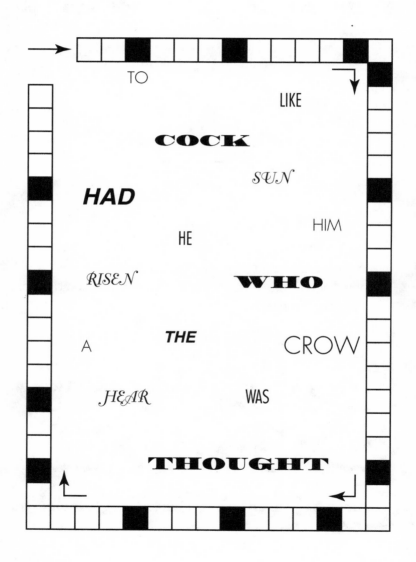

TO

LIKE

COCK

SUN

HAD

HE

HIM

RISEN

WHO

A

THE

CROW

HEAR

WAS

THOUGHT

Find eleven multiples of 7 on this grid. Each multiple is composed of a series of digits joined by line segments (or just one digit). Each digit may be used only once.

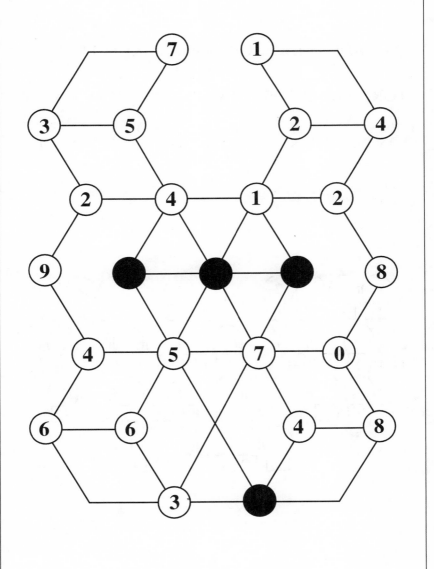

U se the first quote from Samuel Butler to find the second. The numbers under each letter in the second sentence show which word they come from in the first.

THE ADVANTAGE OF DOING ONE'S PRAISING
1   2   3   4   5   6

FOR ONESELF IS THAT NO ONE CAN LAY IT
7   8   9   10   11   12   13   14   15

ON SO THICKLY AND IN THE RIGHT PLACES.
16   17   18   19   20   21   22   23

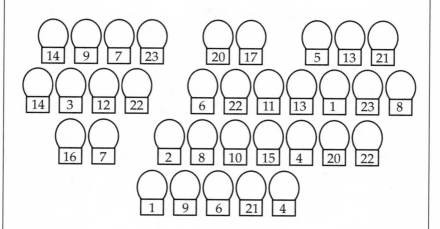

If all the diagonals were removed, how many squares and rectangles would there be in this figure?

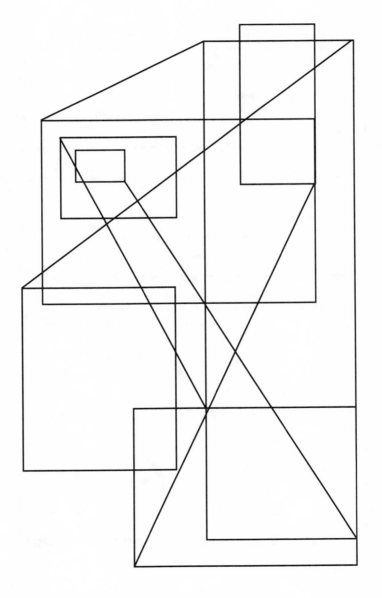

If the rectangles were placed one on top of another, what word would you be able to read?

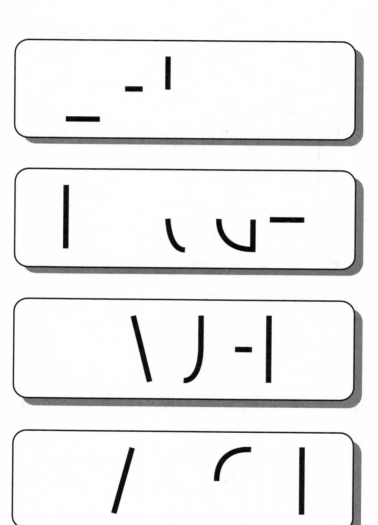

Fill in the blanks to find a Thomas Carlyle quotation. The letters of the quotation are in alphabetical order in each column of the lower figure. Going from left to right, pick a letter from each column in the lower figure to compose the quote. Skip a column when figuring a space between words, and use each letter from each column once. Some lines of the quote break in the middle of words.

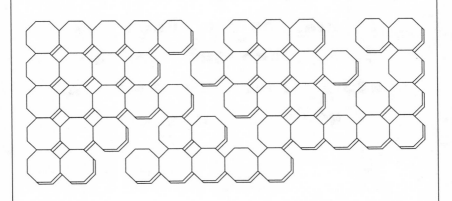

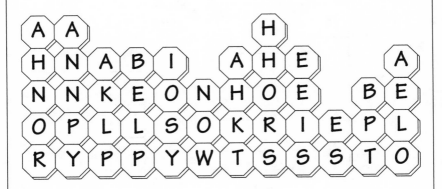

Find seven different ways to resolve this problem.

A foreign tourist approaches you on a New York street and shows you an address on a piece of paper. The tourist doesn't speak English. you don't know any foreign languages, and the address is far away. How can you be of assistance?

Fill in the blanks. Each side of the square is a logical sequence. The arrows indicate a common number.

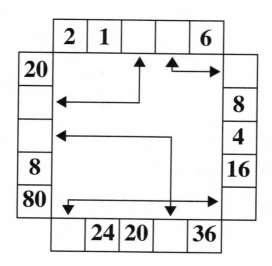

What is the missing number?

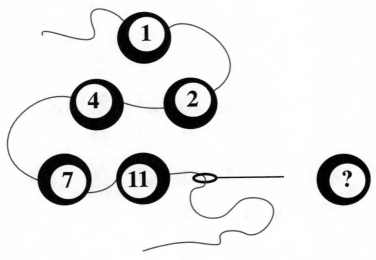

 Can you find seven shorter words that compose the long one below? For example, *intergenerational* is made up of *in, gene, ratio, era, ration,* etc.

...penetratingly...

What is the logical relationship or pattern of the light-face numbers below? Which boldface number fits into this relationship (and thus should be lightface)?

1	**2**	**3**	4	**5**	**6**	**7**
26	25	**24**	**23**	**22**	**21**	**8**
27	**39**	**40**	**41**	**42**	**43**	9
28	**44**	**45**	**46**	**47**	**48**	**10**
29	**49**	**50**	**51**	**52**	**53**	**11**
30	**54**	**55**	**56**	**57**	**58**	**12**
31	**59**	**60**	**61**	**62**	**63**	**13**
32	64	**65**	**66**	**67**	**68**	**14**
33	**69**	**70**	**71**	**72**	**73**	**15**
34	**74**	**75**	**76**	**77**	**78**	16
35	**79**	**80**	81	**82**	**83**	**17**
36	**84**	**85**	**86**	**87**	**88**	**18**
37	**89**	**90**	**91**	**92**	**93**	**19**
38	**94**	**95**	**96**	**97**	**98**	**20**

Connect these ten numbers. Each number may be used only once and must have no divisor in common with the following one. Connecting lines may cross over each other.

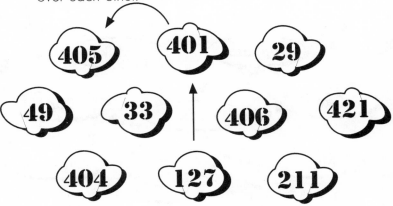

Fill in the blanks. The arrows indicate a common letter.

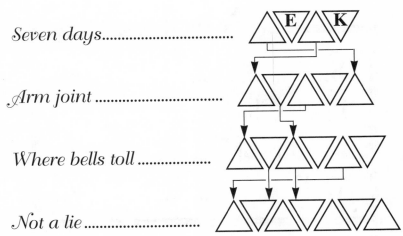

Seven days ....

Arm joint ....

Where bells toll ....

Not a lie ....

Find seven different ways to make pairs with these words. (For example, *cow, calf, kid, cat: cow* and *calf* are the same species; *calf* and *kid* are the young of the species; *cat* and *calf* have the same first two letters).

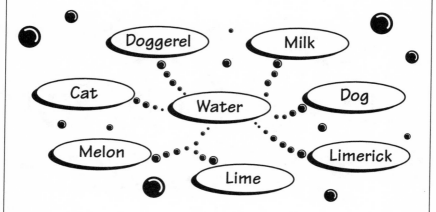

Using the listed items, devise a system that will logically determine the missing price.

Meat

Steak 24

Lamb Chops................ 21

Roast Beef.................. 27

Veal .... ?

If the first square were turned upside down and placed on top of the second, you would be able to read the beginning of a sentence. After you have determined what that part of the sentence says, complete the problem it contains.

				ᴚ
	∩		ᗡ	H
	Ǝ		H	
	ᴚ		O	
H			O	
			H	

T	E		S U	M
	F		T	E
	F I		S	T
T	R E			O
D		N	M	B
E	S		I	S

Find the signs (+,−) that complete the equations.

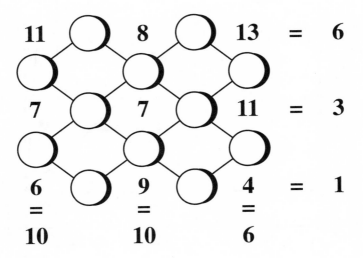

If all the diagonals were removed, how many squares and rectangles would there be in this figure?

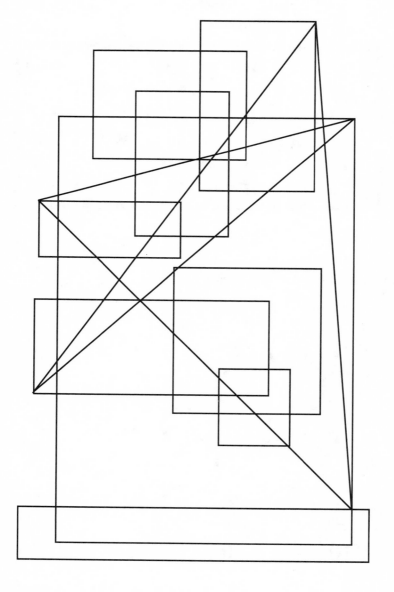

Follow the arrows as you fill in the blanks. Sum totals at arrows' ends must add up.

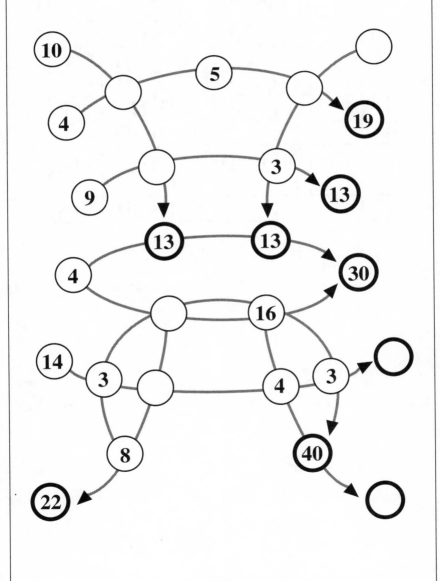

Find nine synonyms of TURBULENT. Each word is written with horizontally and/or vertically connected letters. Each letter may be used only once.

R	G	B	U	T	E	M	P	E	S	T	U	O
I	A	O	N	R	U	L	Y	O	B	S	T	U
O	Q	I	G	R	O	W	D	Y	G	F	R	S
T	I	S	T	E	R	O	U	S	T	R	E	P
O	T	**T**	**U**	**R**	**B**	**U**	**L**	**E**	**N**	**T**	Y	E
U	A	F	T	G	R	E	F	R	G	F	D	R
S	T	R	U	M	U	R	I	A	D	F	I	O
D	E	R	T	Y	L	G	F	C	T	O	Y	U
D	D	F	G	H	T	U	O	U	S	R	Y	S

Complete the equation by filling in the five omissions with 2, 3, 4, 7, and 8. Each number may be used only once.

$$(\ldots + \ldots - \ldots) \times \ldots \div \ldots = 6$$

Use a series of lines to join contiguous numbers whose sum equals 80. Start at "a" and finish at "b."

a
1	2	3	4	5	6	7
8	9	10	9	8	7	6
5	4	3	2	7	9	10
1	2	3	12	13	15	11
5	6	5	4	3	2	1
4	2	4	6	8	10	12
2	5	7	9	11	9	7
1	2	3	4	5	6	7
20	16	14	12	10	8	6
10	8	4	2	6	4	2
4	1	2	3	5	7	9
3	5	7	1	4	6	8
2	7	3	9	2	8	7
1	8	6	4	2	5	9

b

Which game is distinct from the others?

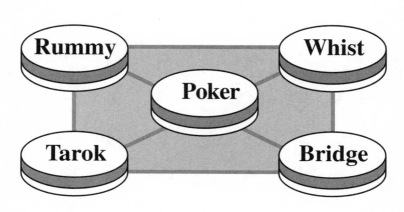

Complete this magic square so that it contains
all of the numbers from 6 to 30. The sum of each line,
column, and each of the two diagonals should be 90.

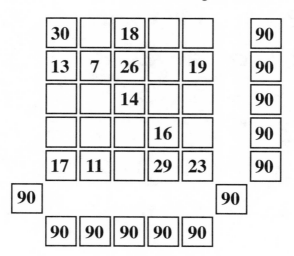

If the squares were circles, the circles were triangles, and the triangles were squares, how many

	circles would intersect a triangle?
	triangles would be within a circle?
	triangles would enclose a square?

INHERITANCE

Grandfather thinks it is time to prepare his will. He has three daughters: Ann, Beatrice, and Caroline. Each of his daughters has at least one child. The six grandchildren are: Frederic, Gregory, Henry, John, Laura, and Mary. Grandfather wishes each of his grandchildren to receive an equal share, but he can't remember how many children each of his daughters has.

However, he does remember that:

> Beatrice has the biggest family.
>
> Anne doesn't have a daughter.
>
> Mary has two brothers.
>
> Henry's brother is six months younger than Gregory.
>
> Laura has neither brother nor sister.

How many children does each daughter have?

Fill in the blanks. Each line is a logical sequence. The arrows indicate a common number.

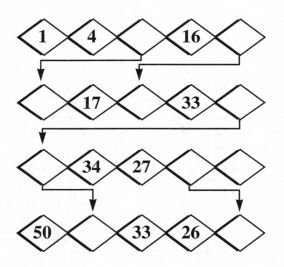

Make seven longer words from *ion* by adding letters to it. For example, by adding letters to *hat*, you can get **t**hat, hat**e**, **c**hat**ty**, **s**hat**ter**, hat**less**, hat**ch**, etc.

...ion...

Both grids contain the same words, spelled horizontally or vertically. If a word is spelled forward in one grid, it is spelled backward in the other, except for one word, which is spelled forward in both grids. Find all the words, and identify the exceptional word.

Y	E	K	N	O	M
B	O	B	C	A	T
R	A	G	U	O	C
T	I	B	B	A	R
O	P	N	I	R	N
P	O	O	E	E	W	I
U	S	O	L	G	A	L
M	S	C	A	D	F	P	I	G
A	U	A	H	A	E	L	U	M
K	M	R	W	B
L	E	R	N	F
I	T	A	O	L
M	O	O	I	A
C	Y	B	L	C	R
O	O	T	I	G	E	R
W	C	A	M	E	B	A	S
N	O	G	A	R	D	V	I
B	I	S	P	O	N	G	E
K	I	T	T	E	N	Y	G

F	A	C	C	W	L	C	M
A	M	O	B	H	I	A	I
W	E	Y	A	A	O	L	L
N	B	O	D	L	N	F	K
A	T	G	E	R	M	N
E	E	R	A	U	M
R	A	C	S	B
W	M	O	S	O
O	U	O	O	A
C	P	N	P	R
B	I	T	R	A	B	B	I	T
R	E	G	I	T	M	U	L	E
U	I	Y	G	I	P	T	T
N	C	O	U	G	A	R
M	O	N	K	E	Y
D	R	A	G	O	N
T	A	C	B	O	B
E	G	N	O	P	S
N	E	T	T	I	K

Words from a Francis Bacon quote are scattered in the frame below. Following the arrows and using each word once, fill in the blanks to reveal the quote.

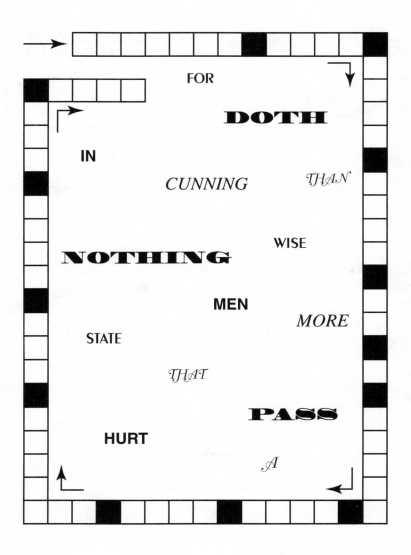

FOR

DOTH

IN

CUNNING

THAN

WISE

NOTHING

MEN

MORE

STATE

THAT

PASS

HURT

A

Fill in the blanks above the clue in italics. Then fill in the blanks of the frame, using those same letters. The 2-headed arrows indicate a common letter.

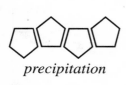

precipitation

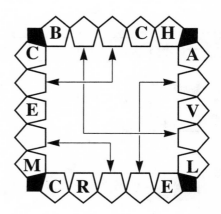

Replace each dot below with either 4, 6, 7, 8, or 9 to make the problem add up correctly. Each number may be used only once.

$$
\begin{array}{r}
1\ 5\ .\ 2 \\
+\ \ .\ \ .\ 3\ . \\
\hline
6\ 3\ 9\ .
\end{array}
$$

Make a word from the letters below, using each letter at least once. One letter must connect to another by a line in the diagram.

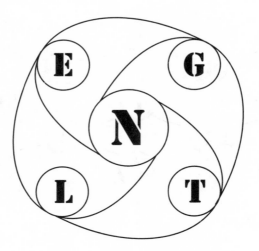

These numbers have many properties in common but do not share all the same traits. Find seven different reasons for determining what makes one or more of these numbers distinct from the rest.

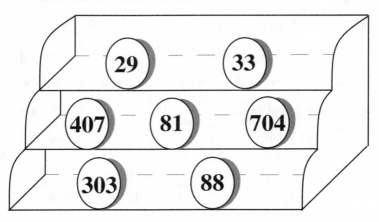

How many times can you read 1464? The sequence is valid only if the numbers are joined by a line.

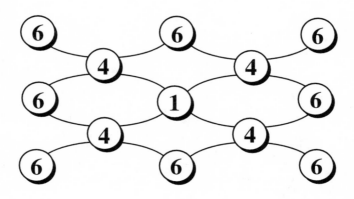

 If this text were arranged alphabetically, what would the 13th word be?

What Hollywood seems to want is a writer who is ready to commit suicide in every story conference. What it actually gets is the fellow who screams like a stallion in heat and then cuts his throat with a banana.

Raymond Chandler

What is the numerical relationship of the dominoes below? Which domino is missing? (Their physical arrangement is not important.)

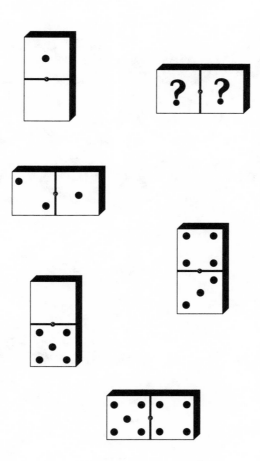

Connect these twelve flowers. Each flower may be used only once and no two consecutive flowers may have any letters in common. Connecting lines may cross over each other.

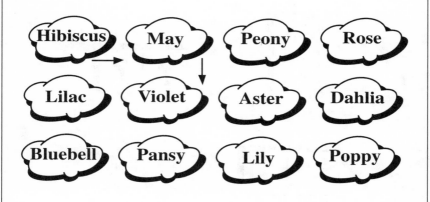

Insert +, −, x, and/or parentheses between the numbers to find the total.

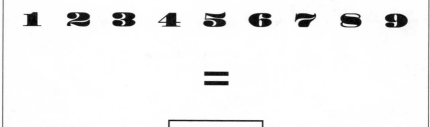

1 2 3 4 5 6 7 8 9

=

29

Find seven different performing artists beginning with at least two of these letters.

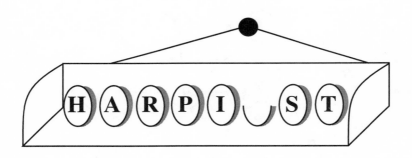

Add contiguous numbers (horizontally and vertically) so that they total 34. Each number may be used only once.

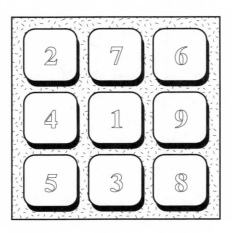

Find ten prime numbers on this grid. Each number is composed of a series of digits joined by line segments (or just one digit). Each digit may be used only once.

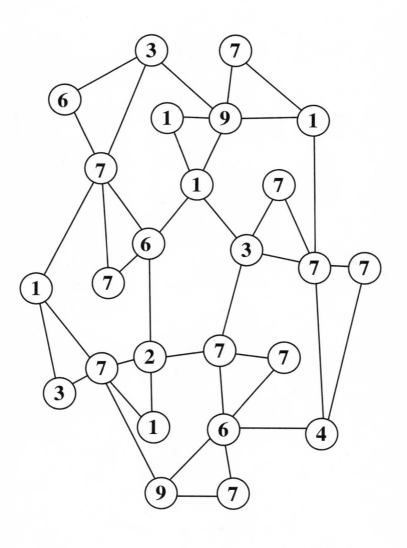

The figure on the left has ten presidents spelled forward or backward, in horizontally and/or vertically connected squares, but the figure on the right has only nine of these same presidents. Find all the presidents and identify the one missing on the right.

A	D	A	M	A	N	T	A	H	A		T	A	F	R
P	S	M	U	M	O	N	F	E	Y		H	O	T	E
O	L	T	R	E	O	R	T	S	Q		Y	R	N	A
A	K	G	R	A	N	T					E	D	A	G
R	T	H	U				M	O	N	A	R	A	N	
R	E	A	R		S	T	R	U	K	R	R	G	R	T
F	O	G	A		M	A	A	M	L	O	T	H	U	S
D	R	A	N		A	D	N	P	O	E	H	A	Y	E

Make seven different sentences using only the words in this quote from Oscar Wilde.

*A man cannot be
too careful in the choice of
his enemies.*

What is the logical relationship or pattern of the light-face numbers below? Which boldface number fits into this relationship (and thus should be lightface)?

8	3	2	75	5	7	1
0	12	8	2	5	26	7
1	6	0	25	4	5	4
1	9	9	2	5	3	4
12	0	5	1	3	62	1
4	9	31	6	8	7	5
8	0	1	2	7	18	3
99	3	6	19	2	4	6
3	2	0	8	18	2	66
4	6	47	1	5	7	3
0	1	5	9	7	17	8
6	2	3	7	8	9	9
1	14	6	2	74	0	11
7	9	4	8	5	0	22

If all the diagonals were removed, how many squares and rectangles would there be in this figure?

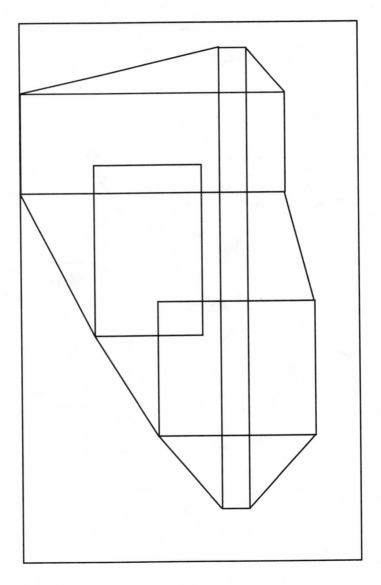

These words and what they represent have many properties in common but do not share all the same traits. Find seven different reasons for determining what makes one or more of these words distinct from the rest.

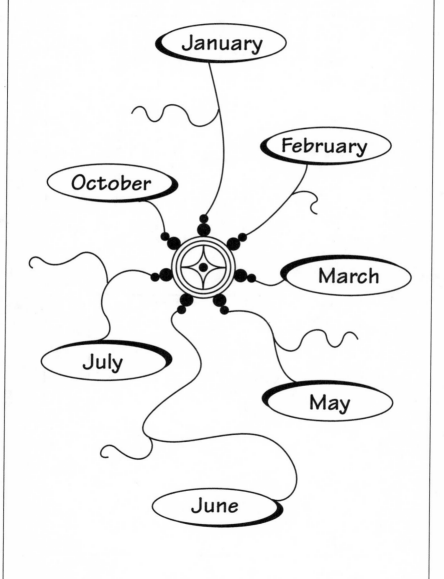

Use the first quote from T. S. Eliot to find the second from Thomas Carlyle. The numbers under each letter in the second sentence show which word they come from.

I HAVE MEASURED OUT MY LIFE
1   2   3   4   5   6

WITH   COFFEE   SPOONS.
  7   8   9

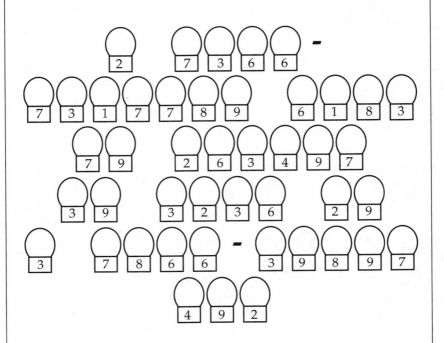

Fill in the blanks to find a Matthew Prior quotation. The letters of the quotation are in alphabetical order in each column of the lower figure. Going from left to right, pick a letter from each column in the lower figure to compose the quote. Skip a column when figuring a space between words, and use each letter from each column once. Some lines of the quote break in the middle of words.

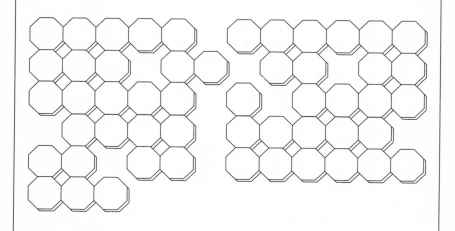

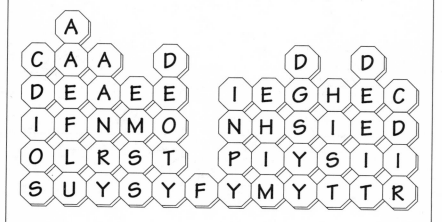

The arrows show the first two crabs in a sequence that is determined by some physical attribute(s) of the crabs. Provide the reasoning that allows the rest of the crabs to be joined in this sequence. Then give the full sequence by number. (In some cases, there may be more than one sequence that satisfies the pattern.)

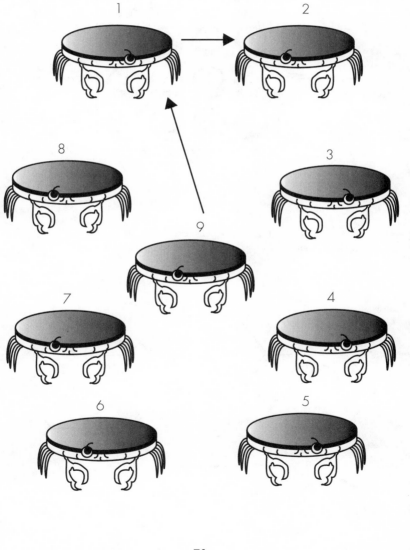

Most of the letters in this square are part of a logical pattern. However, one or more letters deviate from this pattern. Find the mistake.

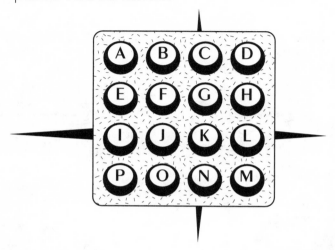

If the hexagons were placed one on top of another, what picture would you be able to see?

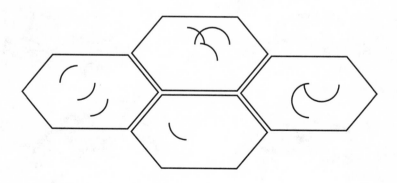

If the rectangles were placed one on top of another, what word would you be able to read?

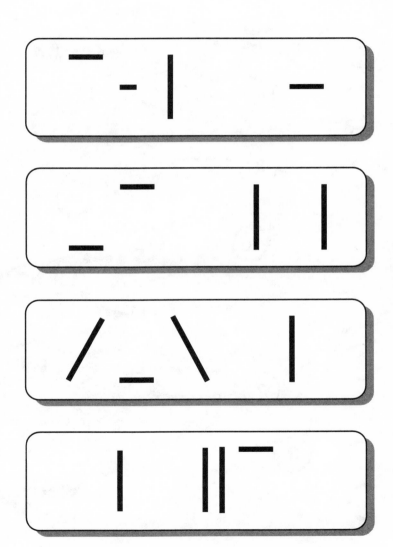

Follow the arrows as you fill in the blanks. Sum totals at arrows' ends must add up.

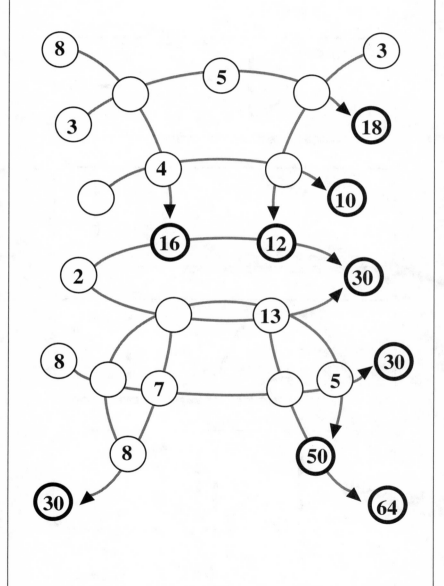

Fill in the blanks. Each side of the square is a logical sequence. The arrows indicate a common number.

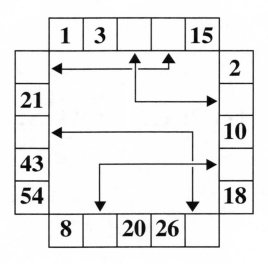

Find seven different ways to resolve this problem.

While shopping, the heel of a woman's shoe breaks off. What can she do?

Can you find seven shorter words that compose the long one below? For example, *intergenerational* is made up of *in*, *gene*, *ratio*, *era*, *ration*, etc.

...thereabouts...

What is the missing number?

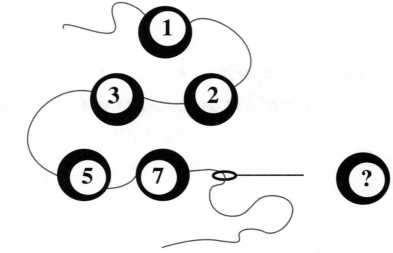

If this text were arranged alphabetically, what would the 13th word be?

Keeping up with the Joneses was a full-time job with my mother and father. It was not until many years later when I lived alone that I realized how much cheaper it was to drag the Joneses down to my level.

Quentin Crisp

How many times can you read 24262? The sequence is valid only if the numbers are joined by a line.

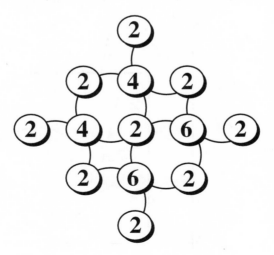

If the squares were circles, the circles were triangles, and the triangles were squares, how many

☐ circles would intersect a triangle?

☐ squares would be within a circle?

☐ triangles would enclose a square?

Find seven different ways to make pairs with these words. (For example, *cow, calf, kid, cat: cow* and *calf* are the same species; *calf* and *kid* are the young of the species; *cat* and *calf* have the same first two letters.)

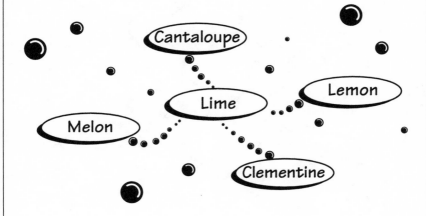

Using the listed items, devise a system that will logically determine the missing price.

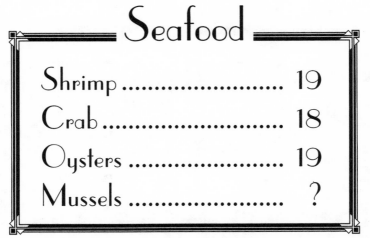

Seafood

Shrimp	19
Crab	18
Oysters	19
Mussels	?

Find the signs (+,−) that complete the equations.

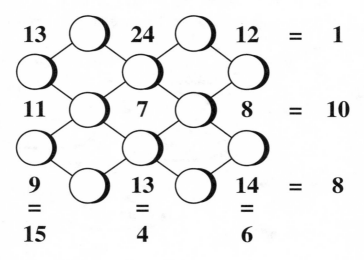

13 ◯ 24 ◯ 12 = 1

11 ◯ 7 ◯ 8 = 10

9 ◯ 13 ◯ 14 = 8

=   =   =

15   4   6

If the first square were turned upside down and placed on top of the second, you would be able to read the beginning of a sentence. After you have determined what that part of the sentence says, complete the problem it contains.

			Ǝ
Ⅎ B		D	
I		Ǝ	
⊥		∧	
D		D	
D		H	N

O	E	U N	
R E	A N		S
E	E N		Y F
I V	D		V I
	E D	Y	I
V	I S		

Both grids contain the same words, spelled horizontally or vertically. If a word is spelled forward in one grid, it is spelled backward in the other, except for one word, which is spelled forward in both grids. Find all the words, and identify the exceptional word.

A	B	R	U	P	T		A	G	O	N	I	Z	E	Y
A	A	D	E	P	T		S	C	R	E	A	M	E	O
B	O	C	A	R	T		C	A	R	R	O	T	X	R
B	A	C	L	I	P		A	S	L	E	E	P	C	T
E	R	L	L	E	T			B	Y	A	I	D	I	S
Y	D	O	N	K	E	Y		B	I	G	T	T	E	
O	D	R	E	F	F	U	S		D	E	W	E	D
A	E	E	Z	I	N	O	G	A		T	P	E	D	A
B	S	I	M	A	E	R	C	S		T	I	R	E	D
S	T	G	I	B					M	A	R	R	Y	
E	R	D	I	A		T	R	B	T	P	U	R	B	A
N	O	W	E	D		I	A	O	S	U	F	F	E	R
T	Y	M	E	R		O	O	Y	E	K	N	O	D	
E	D	E	R	I	T		K	H	R	E	H	K	T	
T	T	O	R	R	A	C		Y	E	R	E	H	N	
I	P	E	E	L	S	A	K		E	P	I	L	C	E
C	I	T	H	E	R	E	O		B	T	E	L	L	S
X	T	M	A	R	R	Y	O		B	Y	B	A	B	B
E	Y	B	A	B	Y	B	B		A	A	R	A	C	A

Words from a Mark Twain quote are scattered in the frame below. Following the arrows and using each word once, fill in the blanks to reveal the quote.

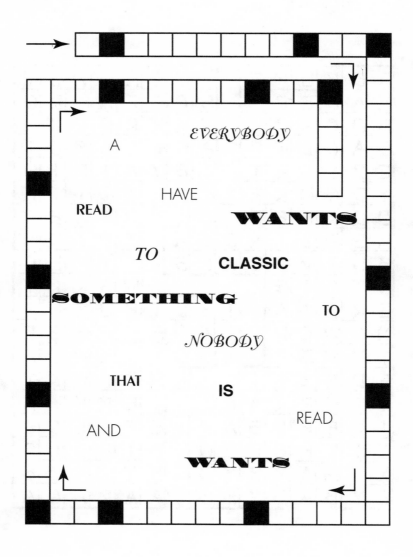

Find eight multiples of 19 on this grid. Each multiple is composed of a series of digits joined by line segments (or just one digit). Each digit may be used only once.

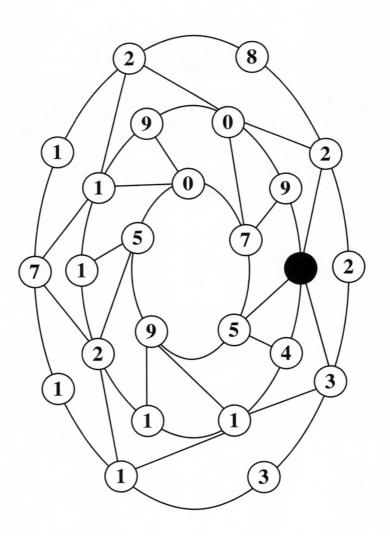

Connect these ten numbers. Each number may only be used once and must have no divisor in common with the following one. Connecting lines may cross over each other.

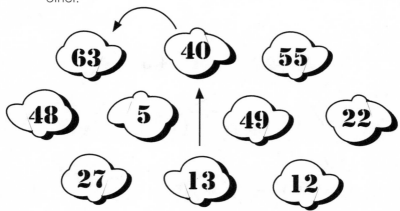

Fill in the blanks. The arrows indicate a common letter.

Ship ....

Bow and ... .

Well-known.......................

Stays.................................

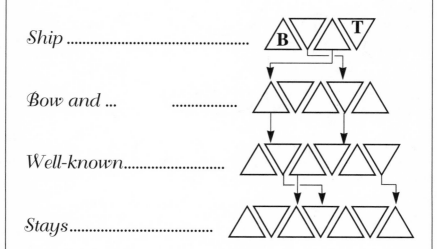

Find seven different professions beginning with at least two of these letters.

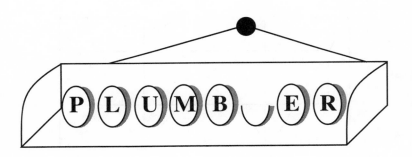

Add contiguous numbers (horizontally and vertically) so that they total 36. Each number may be used only once.

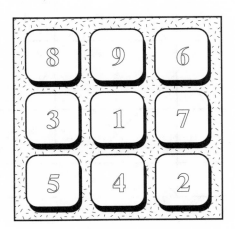

If all the diagonals were removed, how many squares and rectangles would there be in this figure?

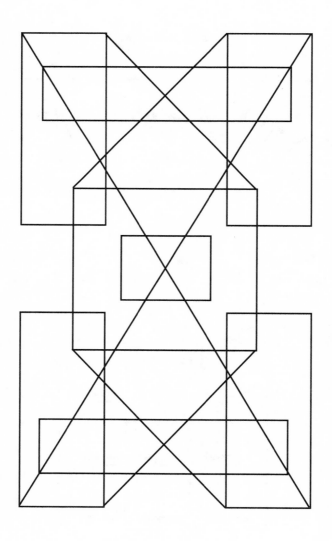

Complete the equation by filling in the five omissions with 2, 3, 5, 8, and 7. Each number may be used only once.

$$... + [(... - ...) \times ... \div ...] = 9$$

Find eleven synonyms of HAPPY. Each word is written with horizontally and/or vertically connected letters. Each letter may be used only once.

B	J	O	Y	G	F	O	R	T	U	N	A	B
L	A	D	F	U	J	F	A	V	O	R	T	F
I	U	G	F	L	K	J	H	G	F	A	E	M
S	S	P	I	C	I	O	U	S	D	B	E	E
S	D	F	G	**H**	**A**	**P**	**P**	**Y**	E	L	T	R
F	R	E	E	C	S	T	A	T	L	E	F	R
U	T	I	M	E	L	Y	G	I	I	G	F	Y
L	K	C	H	E	E	R	O	C	G	T	U	C
B	L	I	T	H	E	F	U	L	H	T	E	D

Use a series of lines to join contiguous numbers whose sum equals 75. Start at "a" and finish at "b."

a

1	2	3	4	5	6	7
8	9	10	11	10	9	8
13	12	11	10	9	8	7
12	13	14	16	18	20	6
11	9	7	5	3	1	5
10	11	9	7	5	3	4
9	13	11	9	7	5	3
8	6	4	2	1	0	2
7	6	5	4	3	2	1
1	9	11	13	15	13	11
1	7	5	3	1	3	4
1	8	9	8	6	4	2
1	3	2	1	2	3	4
1	4	5	6	7	8	9

b

What is the logical relationship or pattern of the light-face numbers below? Which boldface number fits into this relationship (and thus should be lightface)?

60	**22**	**19**	**85**	**82**	**43**	55
30	**22**	**14**	13	**26**	**15**	**85**
10	81	**35**	**48**	**47**	23	**77**
42	**71**	**8**	**11**	**71**	**25**	**15**
48	49	**56**	**14**	16	**44**	**43**
66	**46**	**73**	**54**	**10**	**72**	**30**
47	**29**	**61**	**29**	**43**	79	**67**
67	**5**	**85**	32	**82**	**56**	**99**
97	**71**	**88**	**26**	**68**	**35**	**72**
56	**73**	**19**	**14**	18	**71**	**35**
31	**43**	**72**	**46**	**22**	**33**	**14**
46	**29**	55	**68**	**48**	**72**	**73**
25	**15**	**10**	**42**	**68**	94	**67**
54	**46**	**48**	**67**	**60**	**56**	**47**

Make seven longer words from *oil* by adding letters to it. For example, by adding letters to *hat*, you can get **t**hat, hat**e**, **ch**at**ty**, **sh**at**ter**, hat**less**, hat**ch**, etc.

...oil...

Fill in the blanks. Each line is a logical sequence. The arrows indicate a common number.

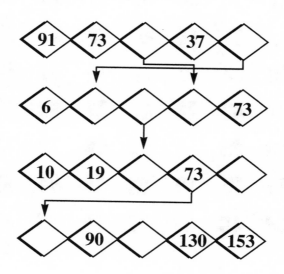

Complete this magic square so that it contains all of the numbers from 3 to 27. The sum of each line, column, and each of the two diagonals should be from 69 to 80.

	14				77
17				27	79
7	22		13	3	70
		15			73
23		8	19		76

69					75
	72	71	80	78	74

Which sport is distinct from the others?

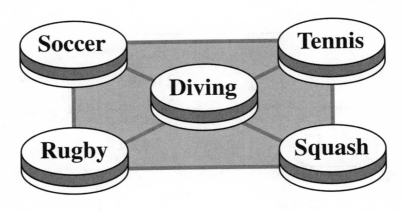

Soccer

Tennis

Diving

Rugby

Squash

91

Make a word from the letters below, using each letter at least once. One letter must connect to another by a line in the diagram.

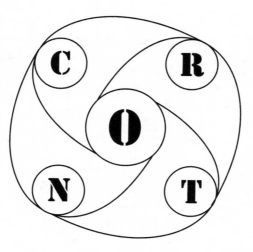

These numbers have many properties in common but do not share all the same traits. Find seven different reasons for determining what makes one or more of these numbers distinct from the rest.

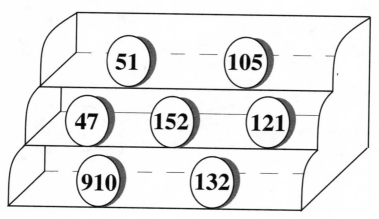

Fill in the blanks to find an Earl of Chesterfield quotation. The letters of the quotation are in alphabetical order in each column of the lower figure. Going from left to right, pick a letter from each column in the lower figure to compose the quote. Skip a column when figuring a space between words, and use each letter from each column once. Some lines of the quote break in the middle of words.

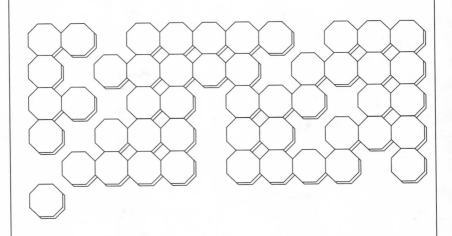

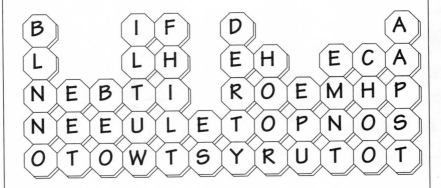

What is the numerical relationship of the dominoes below? Which domino is missing? (Their physical arrangement is not important.)

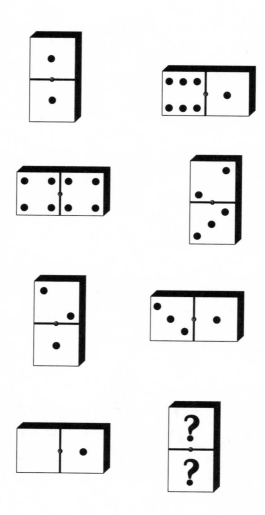

GOLF

Three very busy businessmen want to go golfing together. They have decided to play once a
week, between Monday and Friday, but will
they manage to find a day on their agendas
when they are all free?

Arthur Martin is at a seminar out of
town every Tuesday.

Bruce Brown is on the club's tennis
courts every Thursday.

When Charles Austin comes to the club
on Wednesdays, it is to go swimming.

If Arthur Martin doesn't go swimming on
Friday, he'll go on Monday.

Considering that they all play bridge together
on Fridays, when can they go golfing together?

Make seven different sentences using only the words in this quote from Mark Twain.

All say,
"How hard it is to die"
– a strange complaint to come
from the mouths of people
who have had to live.

The figure on the left has ten sports spelled forward or backward, in horizontally and/or vertically connected squares, but the figure on the right has only nine of these same sports. Find all the sports and identify the one missing on the right.

S	K	E	O	S	I	N	N	E	T
U	M	N	D	G	N	I	V	I	D
B	O	Y	O	R	T	H	E	R	Y
O	G	B	L	A	R	C			
X	U	P	O			V	I	L	B
I	R	G	O		O	C	R	I	N
N	O	D	L		Y	H	A	O	G
G	J	U	F		R	E	F	L	S

K	E	N	D
D	U	J	O
O	B	G	S
Y	O	N	U
X	I	M	
G	U	R	O
P	O	L	O	T
I	N	N	E	T

Fill in the blanks above the clue in italics. Then fill in the blanks of the frame, using those same letters. The 2-headed arrows indicate a common letter.

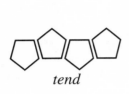

tend

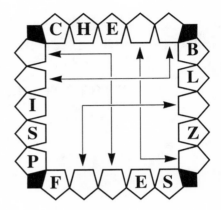

Replace each dot below with either 2, 4, 5, 6, 8, or 9 to make the problem add up correctly. Each number may be used only once.

$$\begin{array}{r} .\ 2\ .\ 1 \\ +\ 7\ .\ 3\ . \\ \hline 1\ .\ 6\ 9\ . \end{array}$$

Use the first quote from Oscar Wilde to find the second. The numbers under each letter in the second sentence show which word they come from in the first.

EXPERIENCE   IS   THE   NAME   EVERYONE
    1   2   3   4   5

GIVES TO THEIR MISTAKES.
  7   8   9   10

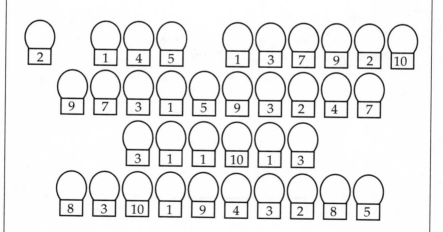

Insert +, −, x , and/or parentheses between the numbers to find the total.

=

60

 Connect these twelve animals. Each animal may be used only once and no two consecutive animals may have any letters in common. Connecting lines may cross over each other.

How many times can you read 353? The sequence is valid only if the numbers are joined by a line.

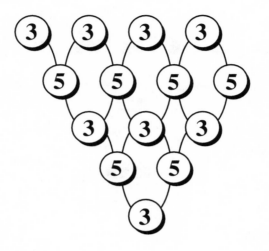

If this text were arranged alphabetically, what would the 13th word be?

Cossar was a large-bodied man with gaunt inelegant limbs casually placed at convenient corners of his body, and a face like a carving abandoned as altogether too unpromising for completion.

H. G. Wells

Follow the arrows as you fill in the blanks. Sum totals at arrows' ends must add up.

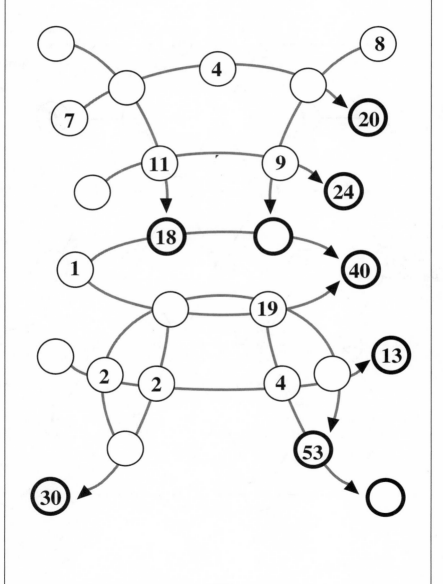

Find eleven prime numbers on this grid. Each multiple is composed of a series of digits joined by line segments (or just one digit). Each digit may be used only once.

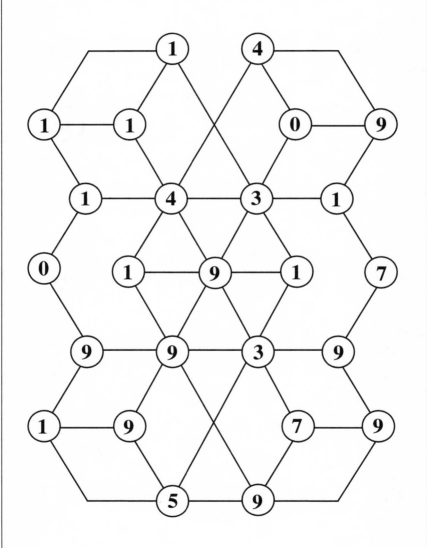

If the squares were circles, the circles were triangles, and the triangles were squares, how many

☐ circles would intersect a triangle?
☐ squares would be within a circle?
☐ triangles would enclose a square?

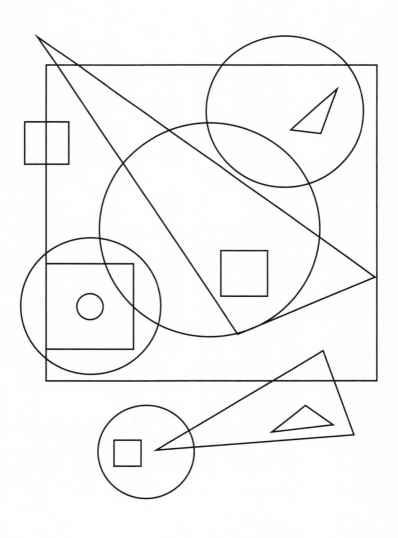

If the rectangles were placed one on top of another, what word would you be able to read?

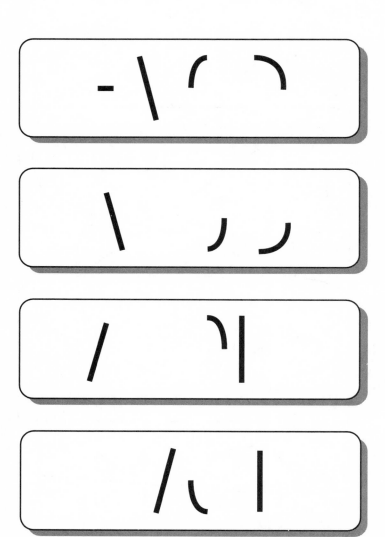

If all the diagonals were removed, how many squares and rectangles would there be in this figure?

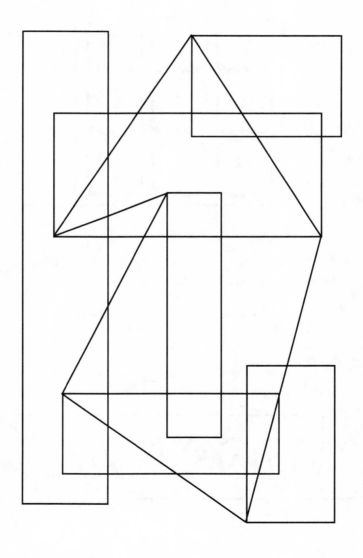

Add contiguous numbers (horizontally and vertically) so that they total 34. Each number may be used only once.

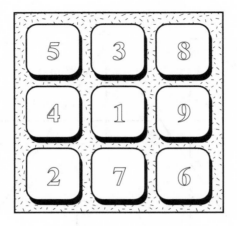

Find seven different sports beginning with at least two of these letters.

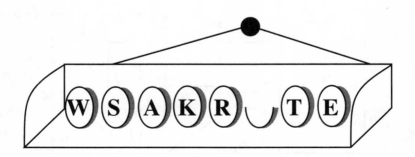

Words from a William Congreve quote are scattered in the frame below. Following the arrows and using each word once, fill in the blanks to reveal the quote.

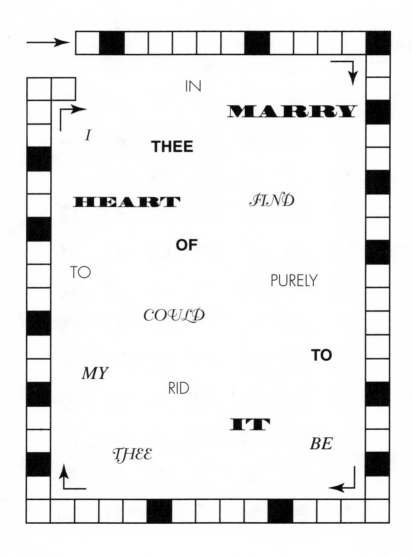

What is the logical relationship or pattern of the light-face numbers below? Which boldface number fits into this relationship (and thus should be lightface)?

1	**2**	**3**	**4**	5	**6**	**7**
38	**39**	**40**	**41**	42	**43**	**8**
37	**68**	**69**	**70**	**71**	44	**9**
36	**67**	**90**	91	**72**	**45**	**10**
35	66	**89**	**92**	**73**	**46**	11
34	**65**	88	**93**	**74**	**47**	**12**
33	**64**	87	**94**	**75**	**48**	**13**
32	63	**86**	**95**	**76**	**49**	**14**
31	**62**	**85**	96	**77**	**50**	**15**
30	**61**	**84**	**97**	**78**	51	**16**
29	**60**	**83**	**98**	79	**52**	**17**
28	**59**	**82**	**81**	80	**53**	**18**
27	**58**	**57**	**56**	**55**	54	**19**
26	**25**	**24**	23	**22**	**21**	**20**

These words and what they represent have many properties in common but do not share all the same traits. Find seven different reasons for determining what makes one or more of these words distinct from the rest.

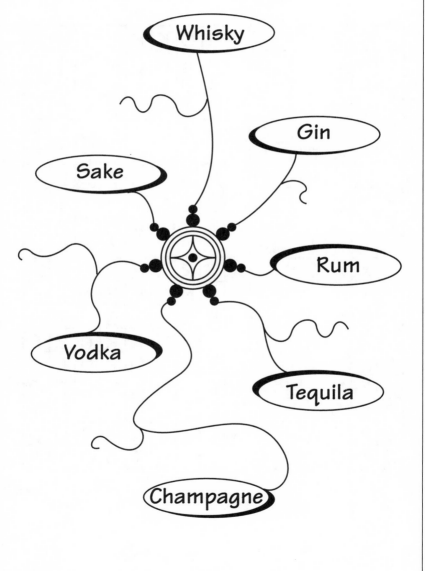

Both grids contain the same words, spelled horizontally or vertically. If a word is spelled forward in one grid, it is spelled backward in the other, except for one word, which is spelled forward in both grids. Find all the words, and identify the exceptional word.

A	F	R	B	R	R		J	O	K	E	R	I	W	F
C	A	E	A	E	E		R	E	K	O	M	S	I	O
T	R	D	T	D	D		K	I	L	L	E	R	N	L
O	M	N	T	N	L		W	I	N	N	E	R	G	D
R	E	A	E	O	O			A	U	T	H	O	R	E
I	R	W	R	P	F	O		I	W	R	R	R	R	
S	M	O	K	E	R	R	H		A	E	E	E	T	
R	H	E	L	P	E	R	E	D		N	Y	T	T	L
E	P	S	K	W	I	R	R	T		D	A	I	A	R
D	L	K	I	A				E		E	L	A	K	E
N	A	A	L	I		W	E	R	E	R	P	W	S	M
I	Y	T	L	T		S	I	N	G	E	R	W	X	R
H	E	E	E	E		R	E	P	L	E	H	T	A	
V	R	R	R	R	D		T	H	P	R	C	E	F	
R	O	H	T	U	A	G		I	O	E	U	R	R	
R	E	N	N	I	W	N	R		N	N	T	R	E	O
R	E	G	N	I	S	I	U		D	D	T	T	H	T
E	R	E	W	I	U	W	C		E	E	A	R	U	C
O	K	O	R	E	K	O	J		R	R	B	O	T	A

If the hexagons were placed one on top of another, what picture would you be able to see?

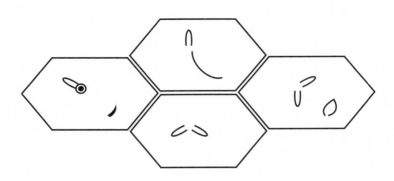

Most of the letters in this square are part of a logical pattern. However, one or more letters deviate from this pattern. Find the mistake.

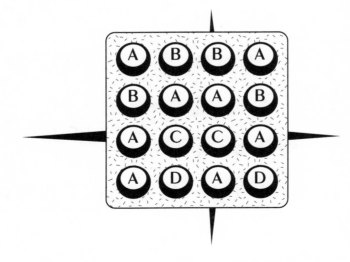

Fill in the blanks to find a John Gould Fletcher quotation. The letters of the quotation are in alphabetical order in each column of the lower figure. Going from left to right, pick a letter from each column in the lower figure to compose the quote. Skip a column when figuring a space between words, and use each letter from each column once. Some lines of the quote break in the middle of words.

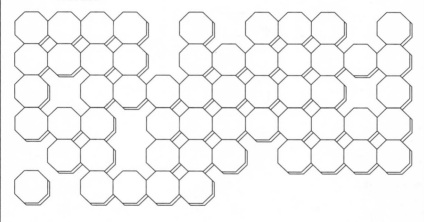

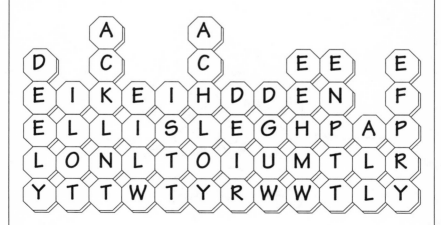

If the first square were turned upside down and placed on top of the second, you would be able to read the beginning of a sentence. After you have determined what that part of the sentence says, finish it by completing the math problem it contains.

```
  S    N    ∀              T    E S    U
     O      ᴚ   ∩          RE     O O      O
 Ọ   Ɐ  ⊥  ∩              F    I N   P L
     Ǝ      N                S    H    S
   ⊥    ᴚ                    A    E    F S
 ∀   Ọ      H              E    E    I
```

Find the signs (+,–) that complete the equations.

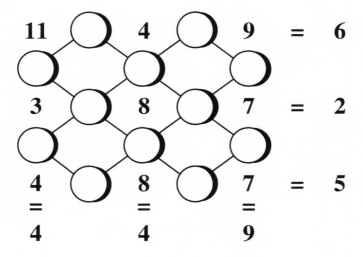

Find seven different ways to make pairs from these numbers.

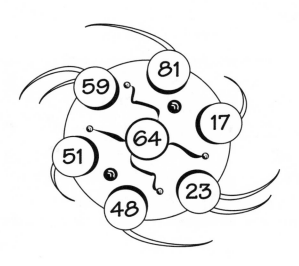

Fill in the blanks. Each side of the square is a logical sequence. The arrows indicate a common number.

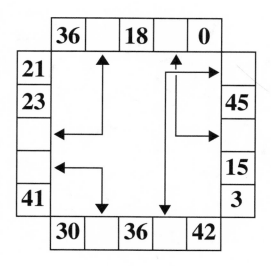

What is the missing number?

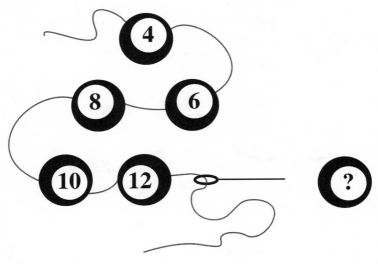

 Can you find seven shorter words that compose the long one below? For example, *intergenerational* is made up of *in, gene, ratio, era, ration,* etc.

...candidateship...

The arrows show the first two crabs in a sequence that is determined by some physical attribute(s) of the crabs. Provide the reasoning that allows the rest of the crabs to be joined in this sequence. Then give the full sequence by number. (In some cases, there may be more than one sequence that satisfies the pattern.)

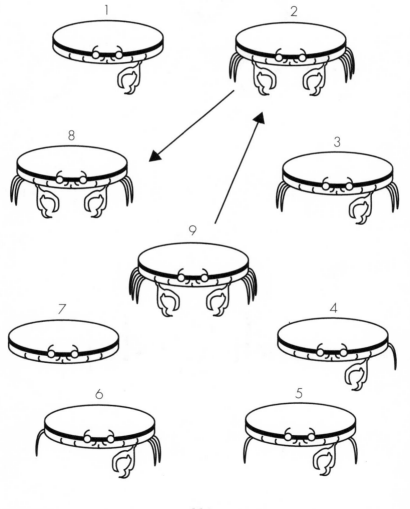

Fill in the blanks. The arrows indicate a common letter.

Nanny ....

Church instrument..............

Physician ....

Sells roses ....

Connect these ten numbers. Each number may be used only once and must have no divisor in common with the following one. Connecting lines may cross over each other.

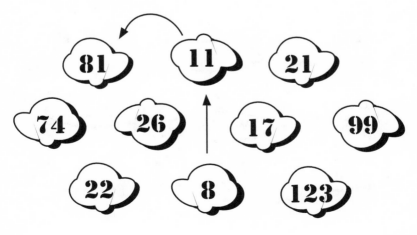

Using the listed items, devise a system that will logically determine the missing price.

Poultry

Chicken Breast............. 12

Duck Filet..................... 25

Roast Pheasant 33

Norfolk Capon .... ?

Find seven different ways to make pairs with these words. (For example, *cow, calf, kid, cat: cow* and *calf* are the same species; *calf* and *kid* are the young of the species; *cat* and *calf* have the same first two letters.)

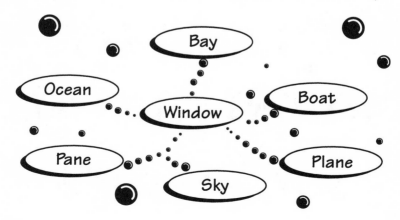

Use a series of lines to join contiguous numbers whose sum equals 80. Start at "a" and finish at "b."

a

1	2	3	4	5	6	7
8	7	6	5	9	11	10
9	1	3	5	8	14	12
10	9	8	2	7	6	5
11	4	2	3	10	13	6
12	6	7	7	7	11	12
11	2	3	4	1	9	11
10	1	5	7	1	7	10
9	6	4	2	1	5	9
8	5	2	4	1	7	8
7	5	3	4	19	18	17
6	12	11	3	13	15	9
5	10	8	7	6	4	2
4	5	6	3	9	8	7

b

Find ten synonyms of PRETEND. Each word is written with horizontally and/or vertically connected letters. Each letter may be used only once.

A	Z	E	R	F	H	G	I	B	I	Z	E	F
L	O	C	G	A	G	F	M	Q	V	E	T	E
L	O	L	G	K	B	V	A	G	I	N	E	I
E	R	A	Z	E	J	H	G	F	D	S	Q	G
G	Y	I	**P**	**R**	**E**	**T**	**E**	**N**	**D**	K	J	N
E	Z	M	C	O	U	I	L	E	P	R	O	F
S	D	I	S	S	E	M	B	L	E	S	S	E
H	G	F	D	T	R	A	S	P	I	R	E	Z
D	A	C	T	G	S	I	M	U	L	A	T	E

Complete the equation by filling in the five omissions with 4, 5, 6, 8, and 9. Each number may be used only once.

$$(\ldots + \ldots - \ldots) \times \ldots \div \ldots = 1$$

If this text were arranged alphabetically, what would the 13th word be?

Skill without imagination is craftsmanship and gives us many useful objects such as wickerwork picnic baskets. Imagination without skill gives us modern art.

Tom Stoppard

How many times can you read 529? The sequence is valid only if the numbers are joined by a line.

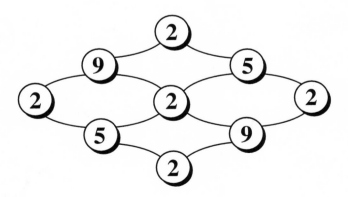

Follow the arrows as you fill in the blanks. Sum totals at arrows' ends must add up.

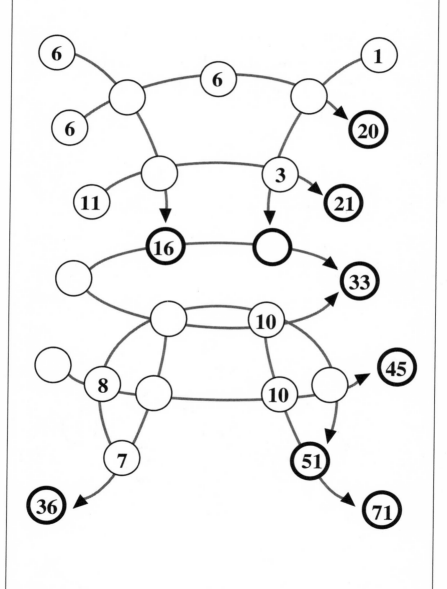

Find six multiples of 11 on this grid. Each multiple is composed of a series of digits joined by line segments (or just one digit). Each digit may be used only once.

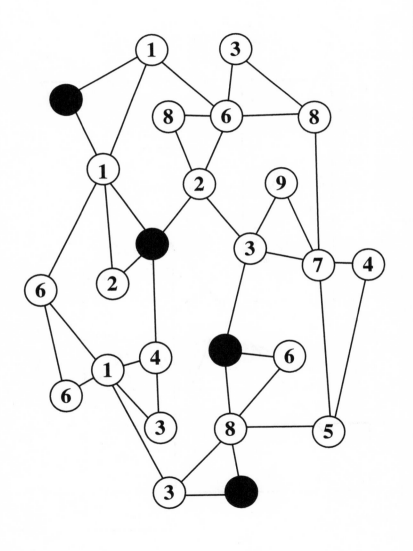

If all the diagonals were removed, how many squares and rectangles would there be in this figure?

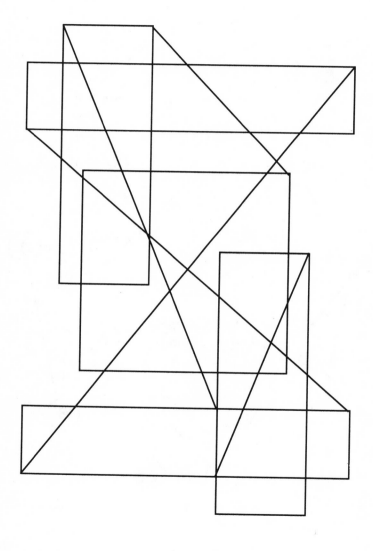

Fill in the blanks. Each line is a logical sequence. The arrows indicate a common number.

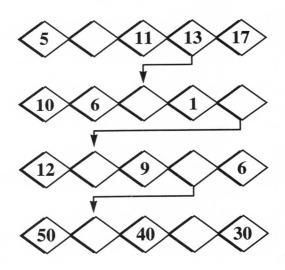

Make seven longer words from *eat* by adding letters to it. For example, by adding letters to *hat*, you can get *t*hat, hat*e*, *ch*at*ty*, *sh*at*ter*, hat**less**, hat**ch**, etc.

...eat...

If the squares were circles, the circles were triangles, and the triangles were squares, how many

☐ circles would intersect a triangle?
☐ squares would be within a circle?
☐ triangles would enclose a square?

Find seven different drinks beginning with at least two of these letters.

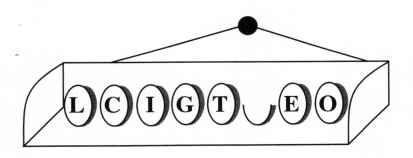

Add contiguous numbers (horizontally and vertically) so that they total 39. Each number may be used only once.

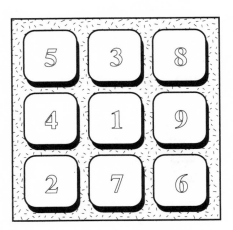

Words from a Washington Irving quote are scattered in the frame below. Following the arrows and using each word once, fill in the blanks to reveal the quote.

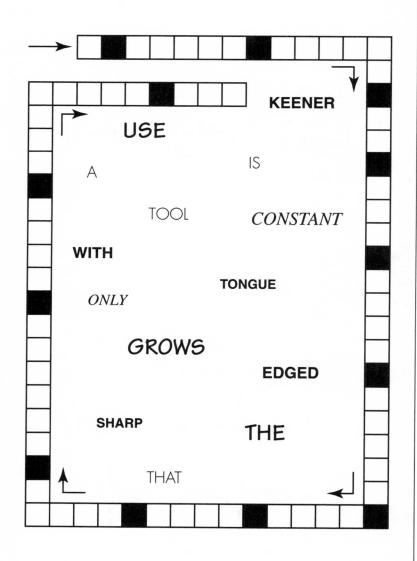

KEENER

USE

A

IS

TOOL

CONSTANT

WITH

TONGUE

ONLY

GROWS

EDGED

SHARP

THE

THAT

These numbers have many properties in common but do not share all the same traits. Find seven different reasons for determining what makes one or more of these numbers distinct from the rest.

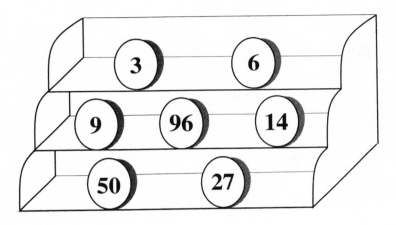

Make a word from the letters below, using each letter at least once. One letter must connect to another by a line in the diagram.

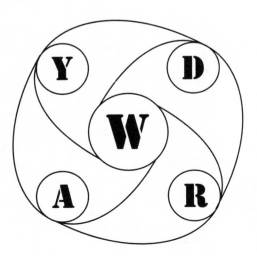

Which animal is distinct from the others?

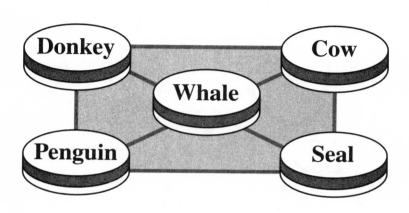

Donkey

Cow

Whale

Penguin

Seal

 Complete this magic square so that it contains all of the numbers from 5 to 29. The sum of each line, column, and each of the two diagonals should be from 79 to 90.

	11		19		**82**
	7		12		**81**
	17		23	13	**90**
					88
		5	29	14	**84**

85				**79**
86	**83**	**80**	**89**	**87**

Using the Francis Bacon quote directly below, decode the Aphra Behn quote under it. Fill in the numbered blanks with the correct letters from Bacon's like-numbered words.

MONEY   IS   LIKE   MUCK,   NOT   GOOD
  1   2   3   4   5   6

EXCEPT   IT   BE   SPREAD.
   7   8   9   10

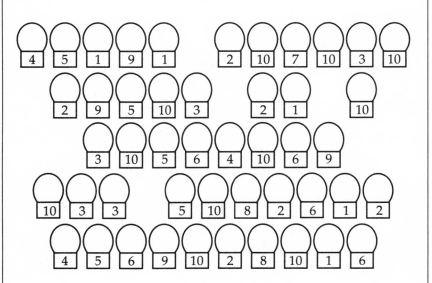

Restaurant

Three friends have decided to go to a restaurant for dinner. The restaurant they have chosen offers a choice of three main courses:

Roast Beef, Chicken Salad, Lasagna

and three desserts:

Fruit Salad, Ice Cream, Apple Pie.

Albert, Barbara, and Christopher have all decided to order the same thing but:

> Albert hates lasagna, and he won't follow roast beef with ice cream.

> Barbara won't eat roast beef with fruit salad, nor ice cream if the main course is chicken salad.

> Christopher will only eat chicken salad if it is followed by ice cream.

What are they going to have for dinner?

What is the logical relationship or pattern of the light-face numbers below? Which boldface number fits into this relationship (and thus should be lightface)?

10	**69**	**69**	**1**	**10**	8	**29**
1	**80**	60	15	12	**25**	**23**
20	40	**90**	**0**	**34**	**8**	24
18	**6**	**14**	**20**	8	**34**	**71**
99	**71**	**7**	**10**	**26**	8	**98**
10	**83**	**78**	**61**	20	8	**3**
7	**9**	**13**	5	**41**	**47**	16
20	30	**9**	**49**	16	**50**	**56**
3	**62**	20	30	**9**	**60**	**31**
10	**71**	**18**	**18**	4	8	34
26	10	**8**	17	**24**	8	**19**
10	**46**	**80**	**90**	4	16	6
31	**5**	**6**	13	16	**34**	**10**
1	**4**	**3**	**2**	**1**	16	**1**

Connect these twelve instruments. Each instrument may be used only once and must have no letters in common with the following one. Connecting lines may cross over each other.

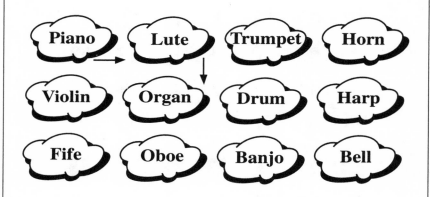

Insert +, −, x, and/or parentheses between the numbers to find the total.

$$=$$

What is the numerical relationship of the dominoes below? Which domino is missing? (Their physical arrangement is not important.)

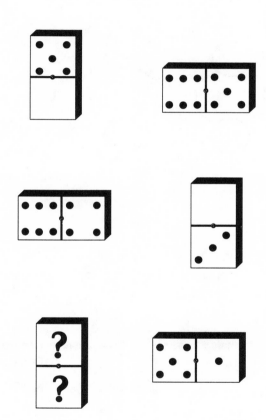

Find the signs (+,−) that complete the equations.

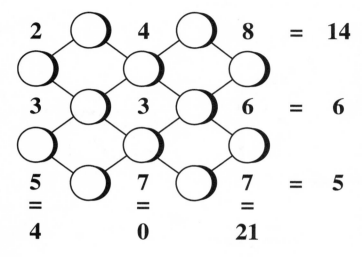

| 2 | ◯ | 4 | ◯ | 8 | = | 14 |

| 3 | ◯ | 3 | ◯ | 6 | = | 6 |

| 5 | ◯ | 7 | ◯ | 7 | = | 5 |

| = | | = | | = | | |

| 4 | | 0 | | 21 | | |

If the first square were turned upside down and placed on top of the second, you would be able to read the beginning of a sentence. After you have determined what that part of the sentence says, finish it by completing the math problem it contains.

Fill in the blanks to find a Samuel Butler quotation. The letters of the quotation are in alphabetical order in each column of the lower figure. Going from left to right, pick a letter from each column in the lower figure to compose the quote. Skip a column when figuring a space between words, and use each letter from each column once. Some lines of the quote break in the middle of words.

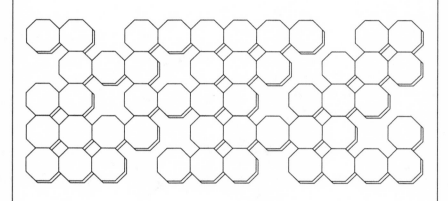

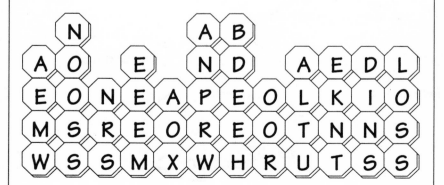

These words and what they represent have many properties in common but do not share all the same traits. Find seven different reasons for determining what makes one or more of these words distinct from the rest.

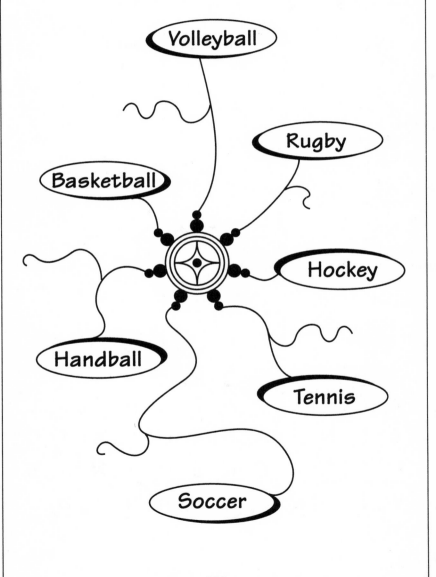

The figure on the left has twelve drinks spelled forward or backward, in horizontally and/or vertically connected squares, but the figure on the right has only eleven of these same drinks. Find all the drinks and identify the one missing on the right.

T	C	R	E	T	E	L	A	S	Y		J	D	A	K
E	L	A	K	L	I	M	P	U	R		U	O	N	I
A	J	K	A	E	R	F	F	O	C		I	S	W	A
I	U	D	B	E	E	E					C	E	E	T
C	S	O	V			A	L	E	C	L	R	V		
E	O	E	R		C	O	F	F	E	E	R	A	D	O
A	D	T	A		R	Y	S	A	E	T	E	T	K	A
G	I	N	W		U	P	M	I	L	K	R	E	E	B

Make seven different sentences using only the words in this quote from Anthony Hope.

*He is very fond
of making things
which he does not want,
and then giving them to people
who have no use for them.*

How many times can you read 531? The sequence is valid only if the numbers are joined by a line.

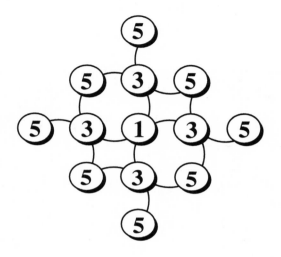

If this text were arranged alphabetically, what would the 13th word be?

Mr. Podsnap settled that whatever he put behind him he put out of existence. Mr. Podsnap had even acquired a peculiar flourish of his right arm in often clearing the world of its most difficult problems, by sweeping them behind him.

Charles Dickens

If the rectangles were placed one on top of another, what word would you be able to read?

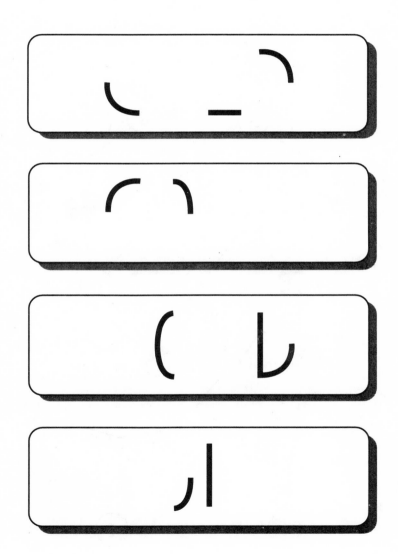

Find eight multiples of 13 on this grid. Each multiple is composed of a series of digits joined by line segments (or just one digit). Each digit may be used only once.

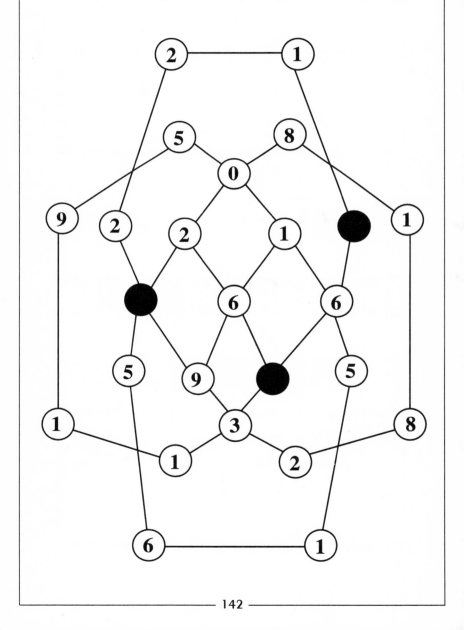

If all the diagonals were removed, how many squares and rectangles would there be in this figure?

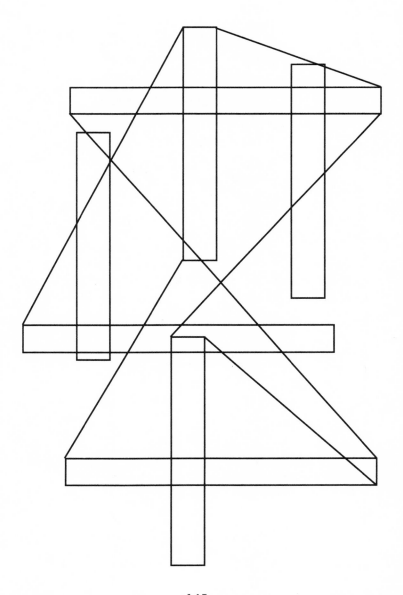

Most of the letters in this square are part of a logical pattern. However, one or more letters deviate from this pattern. Find the mistake.

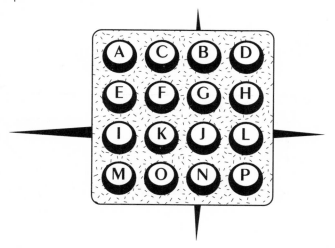

If the hexagons were transparent and placed one on top of another, what picture would you be able to see?

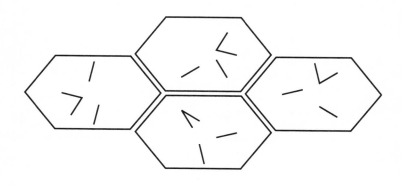

Both grids contain the same words, spelled horizontally or vertically. If a word is spelled forward in one grid, it is spelled backward in the other, except for one word, which is spelled forward in both grids. Find all the words, and identify the exceptional word.

Left grid

C	H	T	A	E	D		
H	G	R	A	I	N		
A	E	L	G	A	E		
R	M	O	O	R	B		
I	T	O	O	T	H		
O	R	E	T	N	I	W	
T	R	E	N	A	E	L	C
R	E	T	E	M	I	T	L	A
B	A	R	O	M	E	T	E	R
H	H	D	F	R			
A	A	N	A	O			
L	I	A	C	T			
E	R	H	E	A			
V	E	I	N	L	O		
M	L	I	H	O	L	L	
A	I	U	T	C	A	I	E
I	O	N	A	R	S	O	G
L	C	G	B	E	H	B	G
A	C	I	D	P	B	U	T

Right grid

C	H	A	R	I	O	T	P
O	F	H	T	O	O	T	E
D	I	C	A	T	U	B	R
C	L	E	A	N	E	R	C
I	B	R	O	O	M	O	
D	E	A	T	H	L		
H	E	R	E	A			
A	C	I	L	T			
N	A	A	A	O			
D	F	H	H	R			
A	L	T	I	M	E	T	E	R
R	E	T	E	M	O	R	A	B
N	I	E	V	B	C	H	B
I	L	G	A	O	S	O	
I	G	T	I	A	I		
A	E	H	L	L	L		
M	E	A	G	L	E		
W	I	N	T	E	R		
N	I	A	R	G	Z		

Add contiguous numbers (horizontally and vertically) so that they total 35. Each number may be used only once.

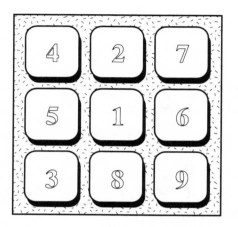

Find seven different vegetables beginning with at least two of these letters.

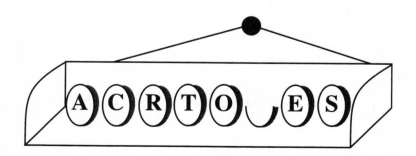

Follow the arrows as you fill in the blanks. Sum totals at arrows' ends must add up.

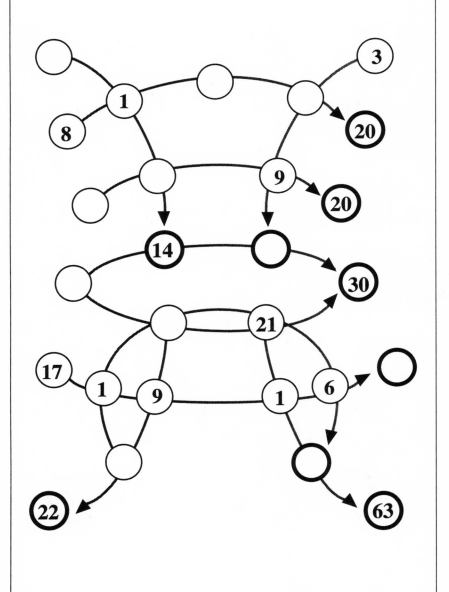

Can you find the seven shorter words that compose the long one below? For example, *intergenerational* is made up of *in, gene, ratio, era, ration,* etc.

...notwithstanding...

What is the missing number?

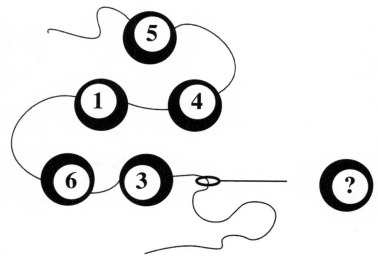

Words from an Aristotle quote are scattered in the frame below. Following the arrows and using each word once, fill in the blanks to reveal the quote.

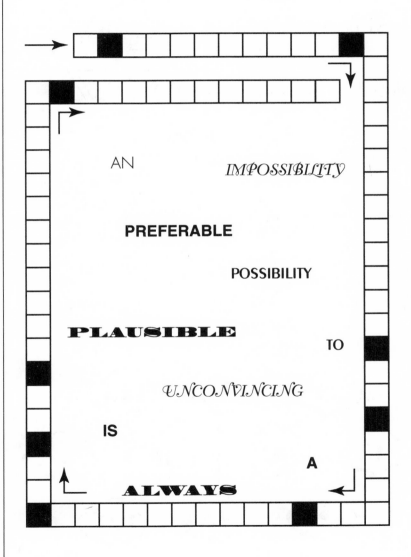

AN   *IMPOSSIBILITY*

PREFERABLE

POSSIBILITY

PLAUSIBLE
                    TO

UNCONVINCING

IS

                    A

ALWAYS

Fill in the blanks. The arrows indicate a common letter.

Large pond ....

Skilled ....

Stage dance ....

Show ....

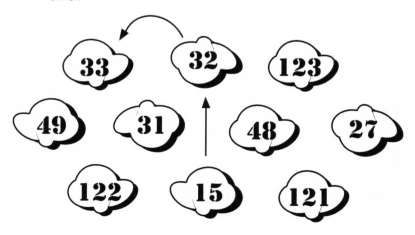

Connect these ten numbers. Each number may be used only once and must have no divisor in common with the following one. Connecting lines may cross over each other.

33 32 123

49 31 48 27

122 15 121

If the squares were circles, the circles were triangles, and the triangles were squares, how many

☐ circles would intersect a triangle?

☐ squares would be within a circle?

☐ triangles would enclose a square?

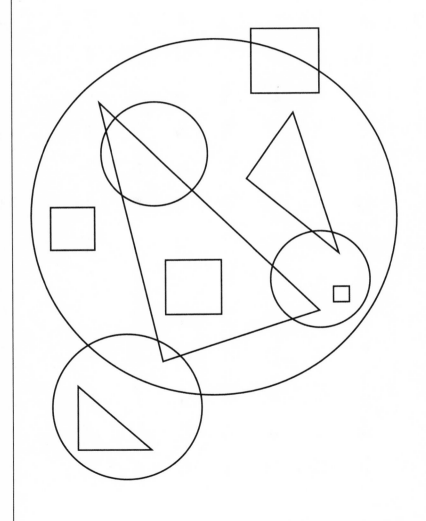

What is the logical relationship or pattern of the light-face numbers below? Which boldface number fits into this relationship (and thus should be lightface)?

1	1	15	**17**	**18**	**9**	**8**
7	**2**	**6**	**5**	**4**	**3**	**17**
16	**15**	**3**	12	**11**	**10**	**9**
10	**11**	**12**	**4**	**3**	**2**	**1**
9	8	**7**	**6**	**5**	**7**	**9**
11	**13**	15	**17**	**9**	**6**	**18**
17	**3**	**9**	**2**	**8**	**8**	**7**
2	**4**	**6**	8	**10**	**8**	**12**
14	**16**	**18**	**17**	9	**7**	**5**
3	**1**	**8**	**10**	**0**	**2**	4
6	**8**	**11**	10	**12**	**10**	**1**
3	**12**	**5**	**12**	**4**	**7**	9
13	**6**	**8**	**4**	**13**	**11**	**15**
11	**14**	**13**	**1**	**5**	**4**	**1**

Fill in the blanks. Each side of the square is a logical sequence. The arrows indicate a common number.

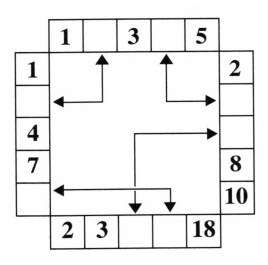

| 1 | | 3 | | 5 |

| 1 | | | | 2 |

| 4 | | | | |

| 7 | | | | 8 |

| | | | | 10 |

| 2 | 3 | | | 18 |

Find seven different ways to make pairs with these numbers.

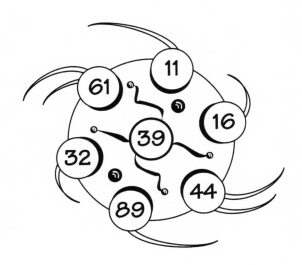

11
61
16
39
32
44
89

153

Fill in the blanks to find a Dylan Thomas quotation. The letters of the quotation are in alphabetical order in each column of the lower figure. Going from left to right, pick a letter from each column in the lower figure to compose the quote. Skip a column when figuring a space between words, and use each letter from each column once. Some lines of the quote break in the middle of words.

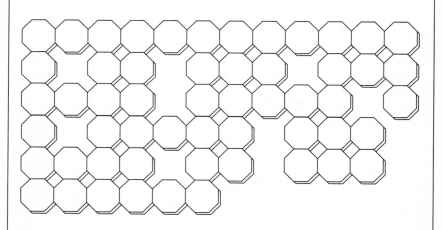

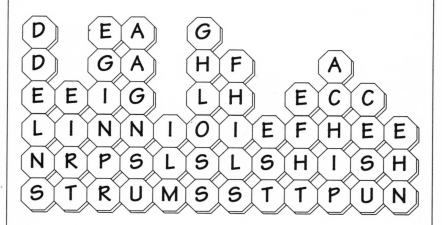

Using the listed items, devise a system that will logically determine the missing price.

Pasta

Macaroni...................... 9

Ravioli........................ 9

Tortellini...................... 9

Spaghetti .... ?

Find seven different ways to make pairs with these words. (For example, *cow, calf, kid, cat: cow* and *calf* are the same species; *calf* and *kid* are the young of the species; *cat* and *calf* have the same first two letters.)

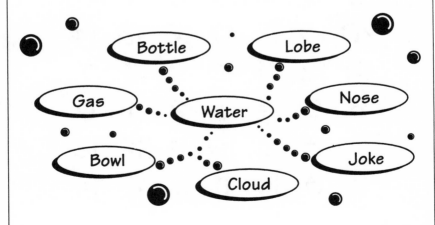

Use a series of lines to join contiguous numbers whose sum equals 170. Start at "a" and finish at "b."

a

1	2	3	4	5	6	7
14	13	12	11	10	9	8
15	16	17	18	19	20	19
12	13	14	15	16	17	18
1	2	3	4	5	6	7
8	9	10	11	12	13	14
7	8	9	10	11	12	13
6	5	4	3	2	1	0
2	3	4	5	6	7	8
20	19	18	17	16	15	14
13	12	11	10	9	8	7
6	5	4	3	2	1	0
7	8	9	10	11	12	13
2	8	10	11	12	13	14

b

The arrows show the first two crabs in a sequence that is determined by some physical attribute(s) of the crabs. Provide the reasoning that allows the rest of the crabs to be joined in this sequence. Then give the full sequence by number. (In some cases, there may be more than one sequence that satisfies the pattern.)

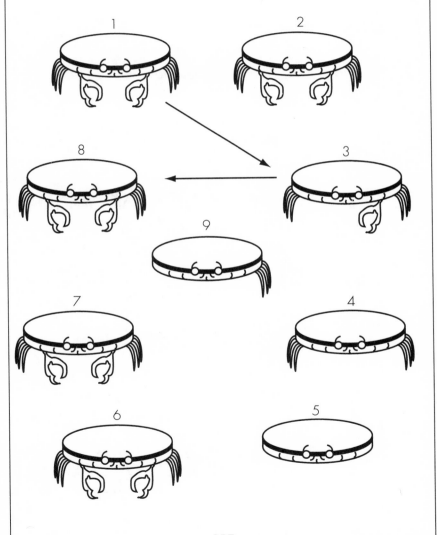

Using the John Updike quote directly below, decode the John Osborne quote under it. Fill in the numbered blanks with the correct letters from Updike's like-numbered words.

THE   OLDER   WE   GET,   AND   THE   FEWER
1   2   3   4   5   6   7

MORNINGS   LEFT   TO   US,   THE   MORE
8   9   10   11   12   13

DEEPLY   DAWN   STABS   US   AWAKE.
14   15   16   17   18

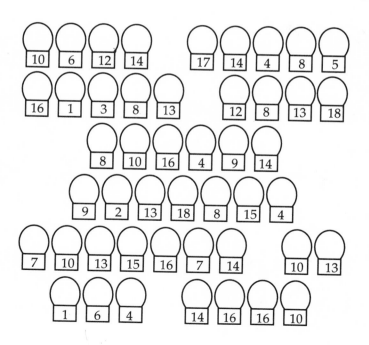

Complete the equation by filling in the five omissions with 2, 3, 4, 8, and 9. Each number may be used only once.

$$(... + ... - ...) \times ... \div ... = 7$$

Find eleven synonyms of CONSTANT. Each word is written with horizontally and/or vertically connected letters. Each letter may be used only once.

D	P	I	M	M	U	T	A	B	L	E	R	C
E	E	D	C	E	A	S	E	L	O	Y	E	O
P	R	P	E	T	G	G	L	K	H	A	G	N
E	I	G	F	U	A	L	E	S	S	L	U	T
N	N	J	**C**	**O**	**N**	**S**	**T**	**A**	**N**	**T**	L	I
D	V	I	N	C	E	S	S	A	Z	Y	A	N
A	A	R	I	A	B	H	G	N	T	S	R	U
B	S	T	A	S	L	E	S	T	G	F	D	A
L	E	E	B	L	E	E	E	E	A	D	Y	L

Make seven longer words from *how* by adding letters to it. For example, by adding letters to *hat*, you can get ***t**hat*, *hat**e***, ***c**hat**ty***, ***s**hat**ter***, *hat**less***, *hat**ch***, etc.

...how...

Fill in the blanks. Each line is a logical sequence. The arrows indicate a common number.

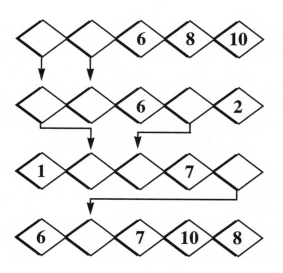

If this text were arranged alphabetically, what would the 13th word be?

The public buys its opinions as it buys its meat, or takes in its milk, on the principle that it is cheaper to do this than to keep a cow. So it is, but the milk is more likely to be watered.

Samuel Butler

How many times can you read 79797? The sequence is valid only if the numbers are joined by a line.

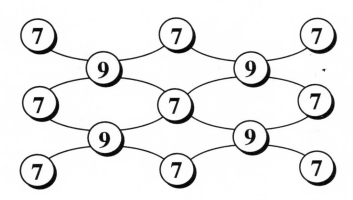

If all the diagonals were removed, how many squares and rectangles would there be in this figure?

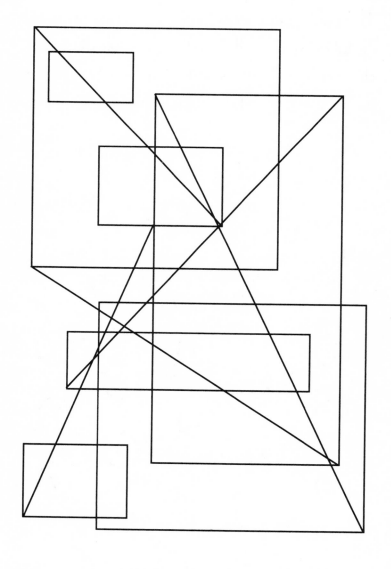

Find seven multiples of 17 on this grid. Each multiple is composed of a series of digits joined by line segments (or just one digit). Each digit may be used only once.

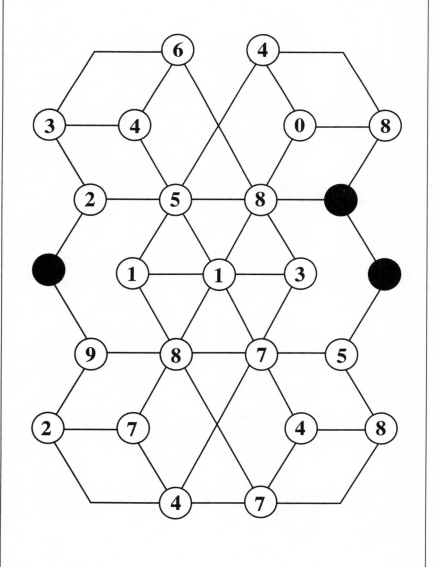

These numbers have many properties in common but do not share all the same traits. Find seven different reasons for determining what makes one or more of these numbers distinct from the rest.

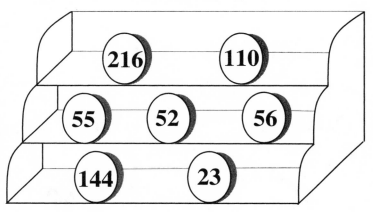

Make a word from the letters below, using each letter at least once. One letter must connect to another by a line in the diagram.

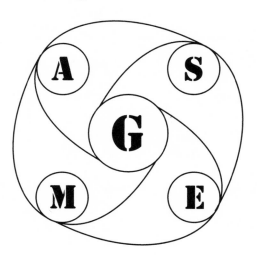

Find seven different animals beginning with at least two of these letters.

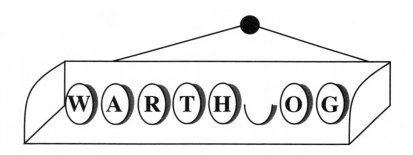

Add contiguous numbers (horizontally and vertically) so that they total 43. Each number may be used only once.

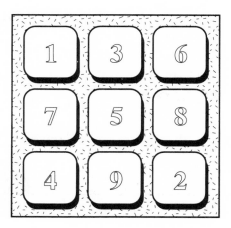

Words from a Samuel Butler quote are scattered in the frame below. Following the arrows and using each word once, fill in the blanks to reveal the quote.

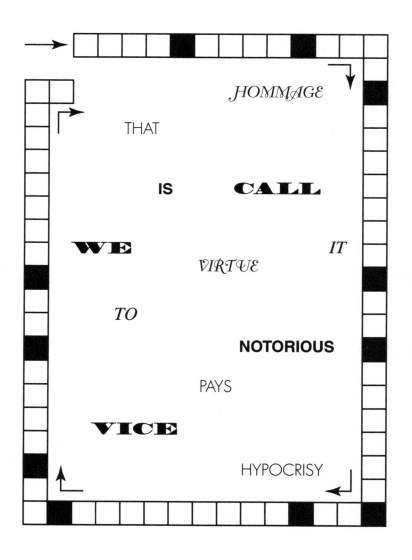

HOMMAGE

THAT

IS   **CALL**

WE   *IT*

VIRTUE

TO

NOTORIOUS

PAYS

VICE

HYPOCRISY

Complete this magic square so that it contains all of the numbers from 4 to 28. The sum of each line, column, and each of the two diagonals should be 80.

21	27				80
13			26	7	80
				19	80
17	23	24		11	80
				28	80
80				80	
80	80	80	80	80	

Which tree is distinct from the others?

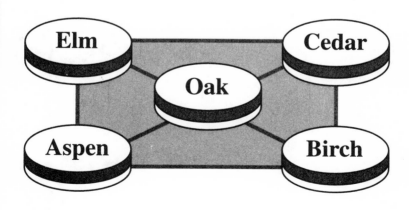

Elm   Cedar

Oak

Aspen   Birch

Follow the arrows as you fill in the blanks. Sum totals at arrows' ends must add up.

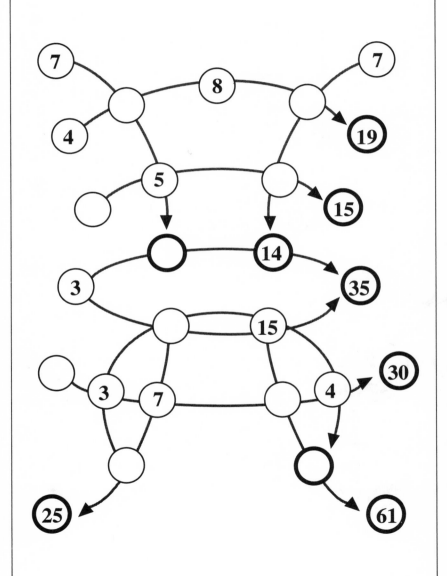

If the first square were turned upside down and placed on top of the second, you would be able to read the beginning of a sentence. After you have determined what that part of the sentence says, finish it by completing the math problem it contains.

	ᴚ	
H		**I**
O	**Ʇ**	
N		**Ǝ**
Ո	**N**	

O	E H		N D
R	D A		D F
O R	Y F		U
R	S T		E S
Q U A		E O F

Find the signs (+,−) that complete the equations.

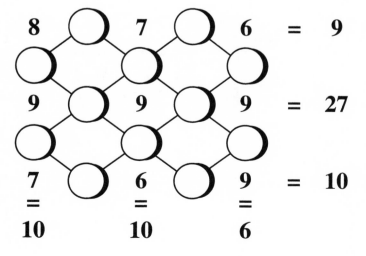

What is the numerical relationship of the dominoes below? Which domino is missing? (Their physical arrangement is not important.)

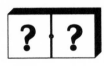

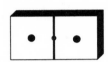

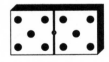

Insert +, −, x, and/or parentheses between the numbers to find the total.

1 2 3 4 5 6 7 8 9

=

30

Connect these twelve herbs and spices. Each herb or spice may be used only once and must have no letters in common with the following one. Connecting lines may cross over each other.

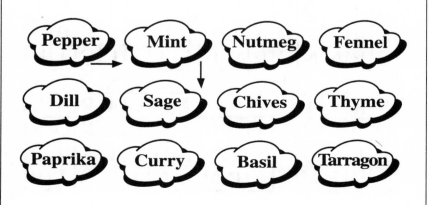

Make seven different sentences using only the words in this quote from Charles Lamb.

Nothing puzzles me more
than time and space;
and yet nothing troubles me less
as I never think about them.

The figure on the left has ten instruments spelled forward or backward, in horizontally and/or vertically connected squares, but the figure on the right has only nine of these same instruments. Find all the instruments and identify the one missing on the right.

H	B	A	O	N	I	L	O	I	V		B	A	N	J
A	R	N	J	R	A	T	I	U	G		L	E	B	O
C	P	N	N	O	P	M	P	E	T		L	C	T	H
O	G	A	A	T	R	U					N	O	E	A
R	R	P	I				I	A	G	A	R	N	R
N	O	D	R		T	U	R	T	E	R	G	R	O	P
E	L	L	U		T	M	T	R	D	P	I	A	N	O
T	B	E	M		E	P	M	U	N	I	L	O	I	V

Replace each dot below with either 1, 4, 5, 6, or 9 to make the problem add up correctly. Each number may be used only once.

```
  . 3 . 7
+ 6 . 3 .
---------
  7 7 9 .
```

Fill in the blanks above the clue in italics. Then fill in the blanks of the frame, using those same letters. The 2-headed arrows indicate a common letter.

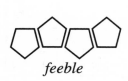

feeble

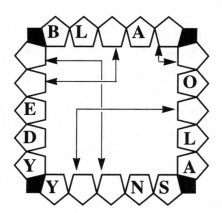

Both grids contain the same words, spelled horizontally or vertically. If a word is spelled forward in one grid, it is spelled backward in the other, except for one word, which is spelled forward in both grids. Find all the words, and identify the exceptional word.

Left grid:

```
R A V I N E
N I M R E V
E N I D E F
F I N N N E
E Q O I I L
N U U A M I N
I I T H R N N I
B N L C E E W I N
U I I E N I L A S
C N N F W
N E E I I
O I I N N
C F I E E
E N I D N U
T E R L I N E
R N O P I N E E
A I B L I N D M
I P N I A R G I
N S N I A L P D
```

Right grid:

```
P L A I N S N C
G R A I N P I H
D N I L B I A A
E N I P O N R I
  E N I L E T N
  S A L I N E
    E I N C D
    N E T O I
    I N Q N M
    F I U C E
N I F E E L I U E
N I W N N T N B R
  T U I I U I I M
  S L W O N N I
    E I F E E N
    F D I N E E
    E N I V A R
    U N D I N E
    V E R M I N
```

These words and what they represent have many properties in common but do not share all the same traits. Find seven different reasons for determining what makes one or more of these words distinct from the rest.

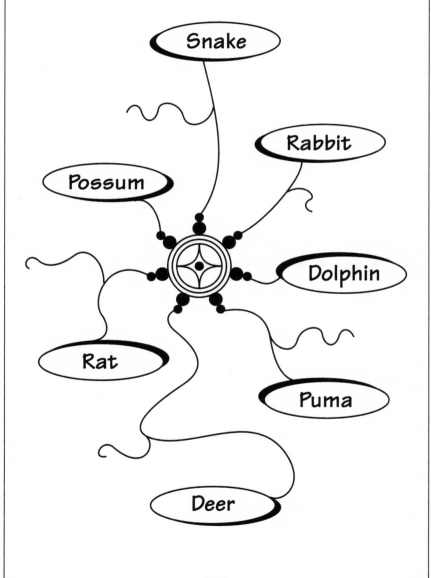

If the rectangles were placed one on top of another, what word would you be able to read?

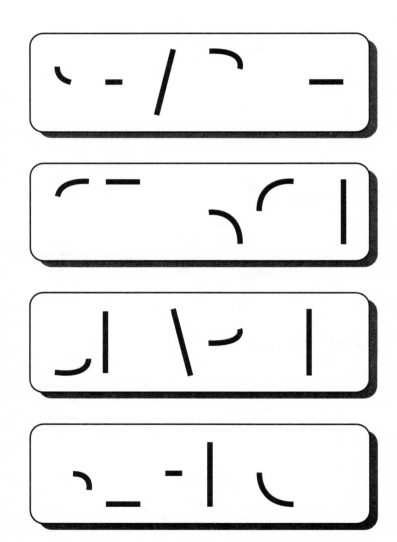

What is the logical relationship or pattern of the light-face numbers below? Which boldface number fits into this relationship (and thus should be lightface)?

14	7	**8**	61	**12**	**6**	7
13	**9**	11	19	**56**	43	**8**
0	5	2	17	**57**	**44**	**9**
18	**40**	11	**33**	**24**	73	**80**
8	3	1	23	**9**	**78**	**81**
12	**16**	67	41	97	**77**	11
14	3	**38**	13	**88**	**86**	**82**
37	**52**	**14**	**30**	5	**75**	**84**
32	**9**	**28**	**47**	**21**	**74**	**85**
13	**8**	**12**	**8**	**8**	89	**86**
18	5	**8**	**9**	**0**	**88**	**74**
12	**4**	**9**	5	**74**	89	**72**
13	**14**	7	**6**	**55**	**90**	**72**
21	**63**	**18**	**44**	19	**69**	67

If the squares were circles, the circles were triangles, and the triangles were squares, how many

☐ circles would intersect a triangle?

☐ squares would be within a circle?

☐ triangles would enclose a square?

Fill in the blanks to find a Jerome K. Jerome quotation. The letters of the quotation are in alphabetical order in each column of the lower figure. Going from left to right, pick a letter from each column in the lower figure to compose the quote. Skip a column when figuring a space between words, and use each letter from each column once. Some lines of the quote break in the middle of words.

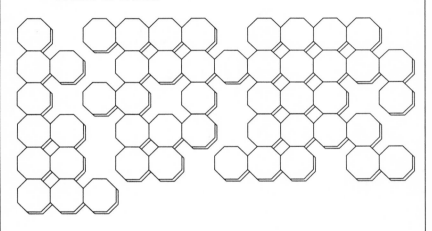

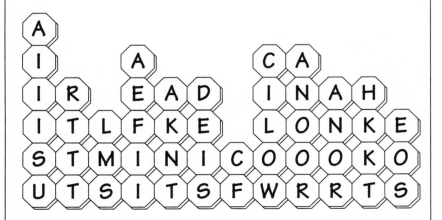

How many times can you read 8686? The sequence is valid only if the numbers are joined by a line.

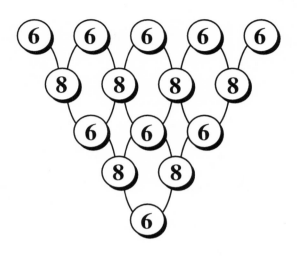

If this text were arranged alphabetically, what would the 13th word be?

I would sooner read a time-table or a catalogue than nothing at all. They are much more entertaining than half the novels that are written.

W. Somerset Maugham

If all the diagonals were removed, how many squares and rectangles would there be in this figure?

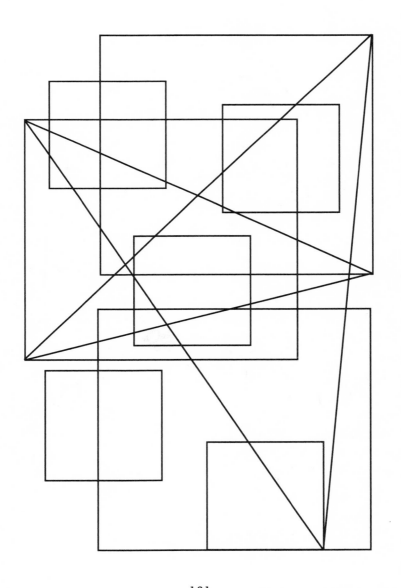

Find ten prime numbers on this grid. Each number is composed of a series of digits joined by line segments (or just one digit). Each digit may be used only once.

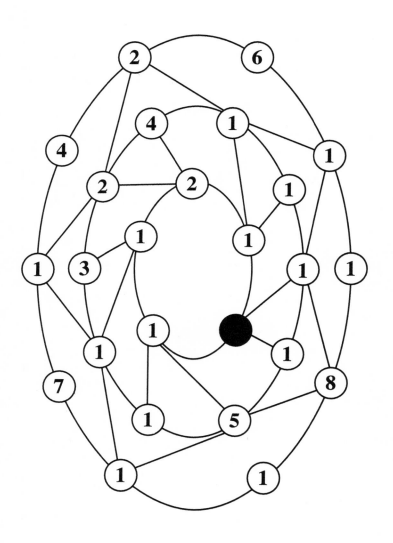

If the hexagons were placed one on top of another, what picture would you be able to see?

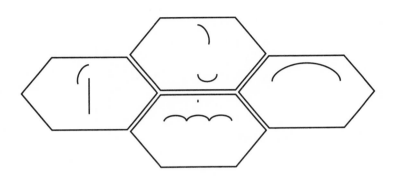

Most of the letters in this square are part of a logical pattern. However, one or more letters deviate from this pattern. Find the mistake.

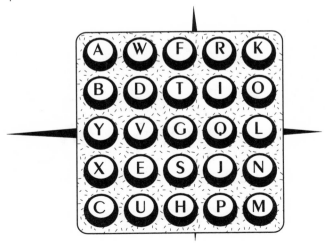

Add contiguous numbers (horizontally and vertically) so that they total 36. Each number may be used only once.

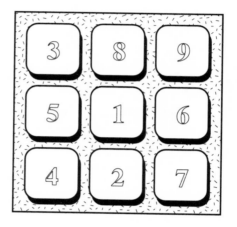

Find seven different means of transportation beginning with at least two of these letters.

What is the missing number?

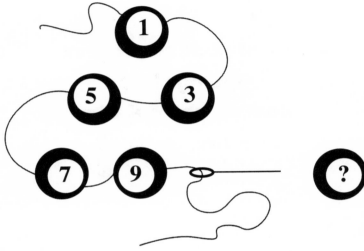

 Can you find seven shorter words that compose the long one below? For example, *intergenerational* is made up of *in, gene, ratio, era, ration,* etc.

...warehouseman...

Find seven different ways to resolve this problem.

One of your employees is always late. How do you get him to arrive on time?

Fill in the blanks. Each side of the square is a logical sequence. The arrows indicate a common number.

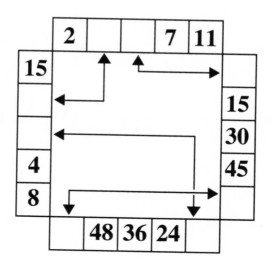

Words from a George Bernard Shaw quote are scattered in the frame below. Following the arrows and using each word once, fill in the blanks to reveal the quote.

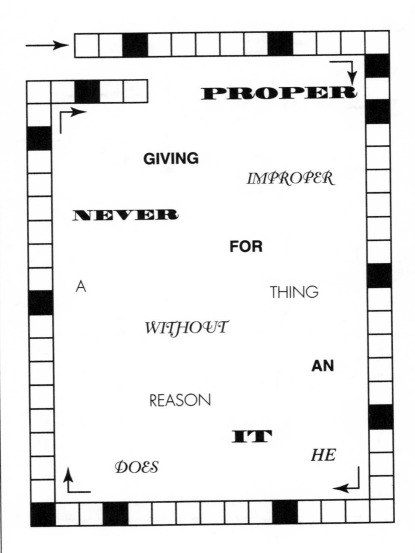

PROPER

GIVING

IMPROPER

NEVER

FOR

A

THING

WITHOUT

AN

REASON

IT

HE

DOES

Find seven different ways to make pairs with these words. (For example, *cow, calf, kid, cat: cow* and *calf* are the same species; *calf* and *kid* are the young of the species; *cat* and *calf* have the same first two letters.)

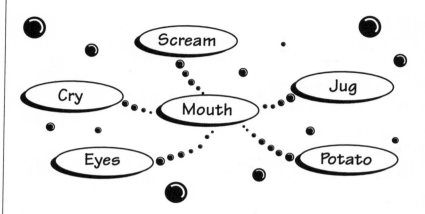

 Using the listed items, devise a system that will logically determine the missing price.

Vegetables

Green Beans 6

Snow Peas 7

Corn 5

Zucchini .... ?

Connect these ten numbers. Each number may only be used once and must have no divisor in common with the following one. Connecting lines may cross over each other.

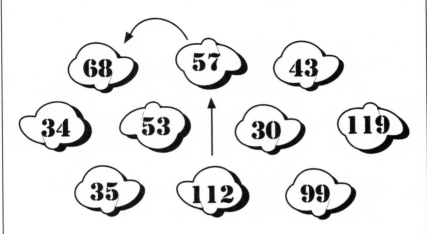

Fill in the blanks. The arrows indicate a common letter.

Utensil ....

On a flower ....

Young lady ....

Humanity ....

Find the signs (+,–) that complete the equations.

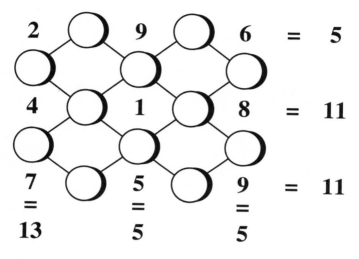

2 ◯ 9 ◯ 6 = 5

4 ◯ 1 ◯ 8 = 11

7 ◯ 5 ◯ 9 = 11
=   =   =
13 5   5

If the first square were turned upside down and placed on top of the second, you would be able to read the beginning of a sentence. After you have determined what that part of the sentence says, finish it by completing the math problem it contains.

O L
M X S
F C D F
H T U
I
U R
D A I N

N E N
F O M N
S P R
O U O
I T I E
S W I S

Follow the arrows as you fill in the blanks. Sum totals at arrows' ends must add up.

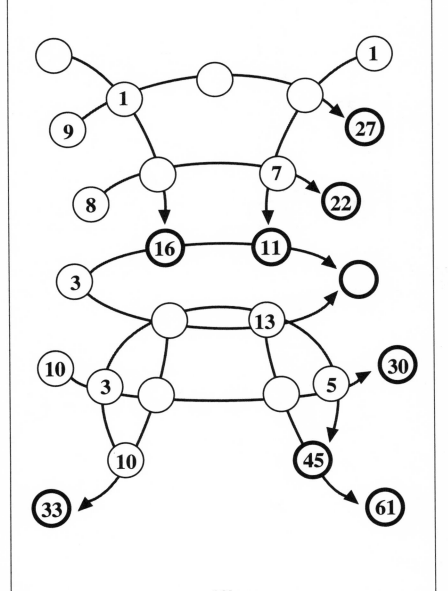

Find eight synonyms of MISTAKE. Each word is written with horizontally and/or vertically connected letters. Each letter may be used only once.

E	R	M	I	S	S	O	P	I	U	T	R	E
R	R	O	R	H	T	V	T	R	E	Z	A	Z
F	R	T	Y	G	E	E	B	L	U	N	D	E
M	L	K	J	H	P	R	S	I	G	H	T	R
I	S	S	**M**	**I**	**S**	**T**	**A**	**K**	**E**	K	L	M
S	B	C	D	E	M	G	H	G	A	F	F	E
J	U	D	G	E	I	G	H	I	J	K	L	M
M	O	I	U	Y	S	C	O	N	S	T	R	U
I	S	U	N	D	E	R	S	T	A	N	D	E

Complete the equation by filling in the five omissions with 1, 2, 5, 8, and 9. Each number may be used only once.

$$[\ldots + \ldots - (\ldots \times \ldots)] \div \ldots = 6$$

Using the Logan P. Smith quote directly below, decode the Samuel Butler quote under it. Fill in the numbered blanks with the correct letters from Smith's like-numbered words.

PEOPLE   SAY   THAT   LIFE   IS   THE   THING,
   1   2   3   4   5   6   7

BUT   I   PREFER   READING.
  8   9   10   11

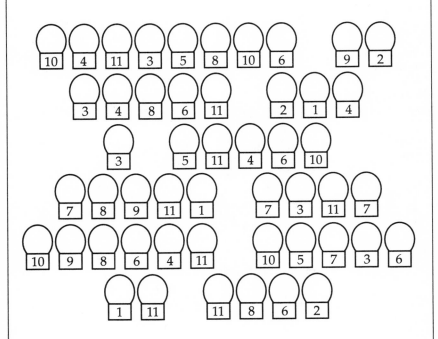

Which fruit is distinct from the others?

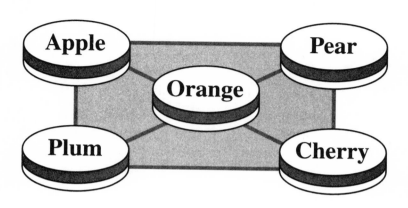

Apple

Pear

Orange

Plum

Cherry

Complete this magic square so that it contains all of the numbers from 6 to 30. The sum of each line, column, and each of the two diagonals should be 90.

17			13	30	**90**
11	28				**90**
		14		18	**90**
29			25		**90**
23			19	6	**90**

90   **90**

| **90** | **90** | **90** | **90** | **90** |

Fill in the blanks. Each line is a logical sequence. The arrows indicate a common number.

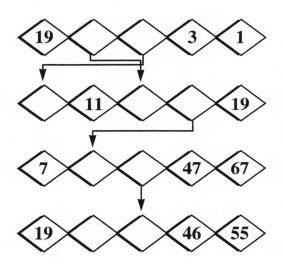

Make seven longer words from *sea* by adding letters to it. For example, by adding letters to *hat*, you can get *t*hat, *hate*, *ch*at*ty*, *s*hat*ter*, *hat**less**, *hat**ch**, etc.

What is the logical relationship or pattern of the light-face numbers below? Which boldface number fits into this relationship (and thus should be lightface)?

1	**2**	**3**	4	**5**	**6**	7
26	**25**	**24**	**23**	22	**21**	**8**
27	**39**	**40**	**41**	**42**	**43**	**9**
28	**44**	**45**	46	**47**	**48**	**10**
29	**49**	**50**	**51**	**52**	**53**	11
30	**54**	**55**	56	**57**	**58**	**12**
31	**59**	**60**	**61**	**62**	**63**	**13**
32	**64**	**65**	**66**	67	**68**	**14**
33	**69**	**70**	**71**	**72**	**73**	**15**
34	**74**	**75**	**76**	**77**	**78**	16
35	79	**80**	**81**	**82**	**83**	**17**
36	**84**	**85**	**86**	**87**	**88**	**18**
37	**89**	**90**	**91**	92	**93**	**19**
38	**94**	**95**	**96**	**97**	**98**	**20**

Use a series of lines to join contiguous numbers whose sum equals 210. Start at "a" and finish at "b."

a

10	9	8	7	6	5	4
3	2	1	0	2	3	4
5	6	7	8	9	10	11
12	13	14	15	16	17	18
20	22	24	26	28	30	32
34	36	32	30	28	24	22
20	18	16	14	12	10	8
6	4	2	0	1	3	5
7	8	9	11	12	13	14
15	1	2	3	4	5	7
11	13	15	8	5	15	9
7	8	9	10	20	11	13
6	5	4	3	9	2	1
13	11	9	7	1	5	3

b

FAMILY REUNION

Here is a strange type of family reunion. The Brown family has decided that instead of reuniting as many members of the family as possible, they would try to represent as many family relations with as few people as they could. Therefore, when the time for the reunion comes around, few of them are present but there are nonetheless a father, a mother, a son, a daughter, a brother, a sister, a nephew, a niece, an aunt, an uncle, and a cousin of either sex.

All of them have a common ancestor, and there are no consanguineous marriages.

The number of people present is the exact minimum needed in order to represent those relations.

How many of them are there?

Make a word from the letters below, using each letter at least once. One letter must connect to another by a line in the diagram.

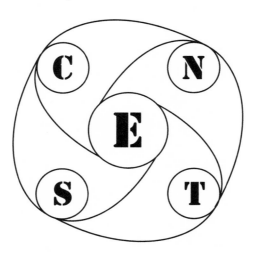

These numbers have many properties in common but do not share all the same traits. Find seven different reasons for determining what makes one or more of these numbers distinct from the rest.

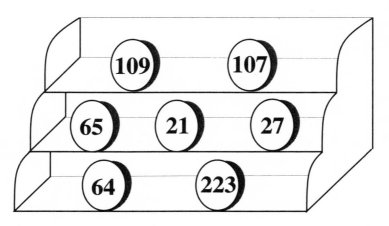

If all the diagonals were removed, how many squares and rectangles would there be in this figure?

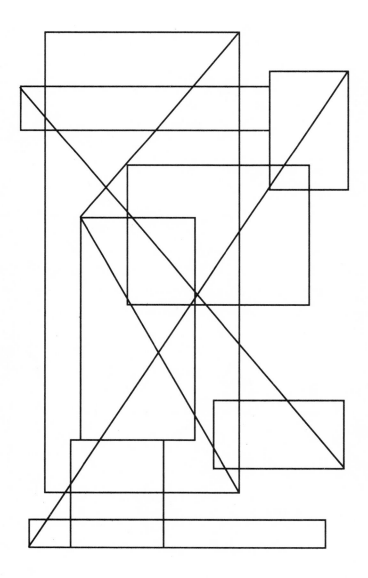

Thursday

Both grids contain the same words, spelled horizontally or vertically. If a word is spelled forward in one grid, it is spelled backward in the other, except for one word, which is spelled forward in both grids. Find all the words, and identify the exceptional word.

Left grid:

```
H E L B A T
R M O T I F
E E R O D A
T S T A M P
A S N A E M
L S H A D O W
P R E L E E P D
L B L O W E R O U
O R E T T U C G T
U N R L N
G O E A W
H I W T O
R S O I L
E E M N C D
P D R E D G E
A E N I G N E R
E A B O L I S H
R S P I N N E R
P A C K E R T O
```

Right grid:

```
E N G I N E R L
R E W O L B E A
C U T T E R A T
E G D E R D P E
M E A N S E R
G E N M R T
S I O G C
I T W G L
O A E O O
N L R D W
P E E L E R Y R N
H S I L O B A G H
S P I N N E R G
W O D A H S U
F I T O M O
A D O R E L
P M A T S P
R E K C A P
T A B L E A
```

Fill in the blanks to find a Rose Macaulay quotation. The letters of the quotation are in alphabetical order in each column of the lower figure. Going from left to right, pick a letter from each column in the lower figure to compose the quote. Skip a column when figuring a space between words, and use each letter from each column once. Some lines of the quote break in the middle of words.

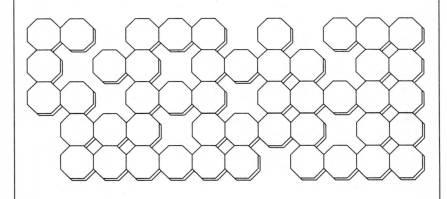

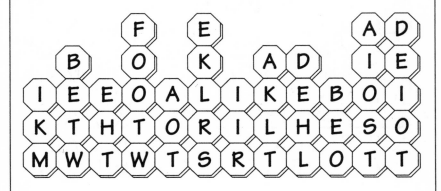

If the squares were circles, the circles were triangles, and the triangles were squares, how many

circles would intersect a triangle?

squares would be within a circle?

triangles would enclose a square?

Fill in the blanks above the clue in italics. Then fill in the blanks of the frame, using those same letters. The 2-headed arrows indicate a common letter.

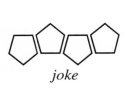

joke

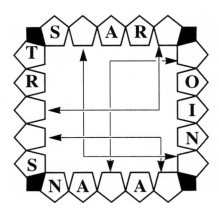

Replace each dot below with either 2, 4, 5, 6, or 7 to make the problem add up correctly. Each number may be used only once.

$$
\begin{array}{r}
6\ .\ .\ 1 \\
+\ 7\ 9\ 7\ . \\
\hline
1\ 4\ .\ 9\ . \\
\end{array}
$$

What is the numerical relationship of the dominoes below? Which domino is missing? (Their physical arrangement is not important.)

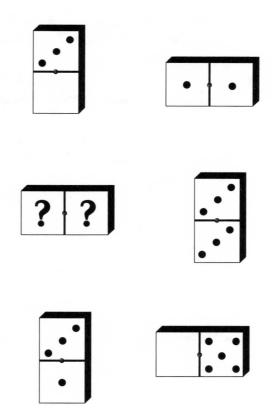

Connect these twelve fruits. Each fruit may be used only once and must have no letters in common with the following one. Connecting lines may cross over each other.

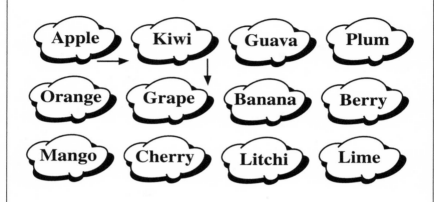

Insert +, −, x, and/or parentheses between the numbers to find the total.

1 2 3 4 5 6 7 8 9

=

80

The figure on the left has eleven authors spelled forward or backward, in horizontally and/or vertically connected squares, but the figure on the right has only ten of these same authors. Find all the authors and identify the one missing on the right.

W	B	E	C	K	E	T	T	T	W		L	A	N	G
A	L	A	N	G	N	I	A	W	I		A	W	I	M
U	E	L	I	O	T	A	E	D	L		M	T	L	A
G	A	H	N	E	K	I					I	W	D	N
H	R	D	Y				T	T	S	S	A	E	N	
A	K	I	A		B	E	C	K	E	A	N	I	N	E
S	S	I	M		H	G	U	A	L	K	H	A	I	K
M	A	N	N		E	L	I	O	T	I	A	R	D	Y

Make seven different sentences using only the words in this quote from Oscar Wilde.

*It is only shallow people
who do not judge
by appearances.*

The arrows show the first two crabs in a sequence that is determined by some physical attribute(s) of the crabs. Provide the reasoning that allows the rest of the crabs to be joined in this sequence. Then give the full sequence by number. (In some cases, there may be more than one sequence that satisfies the pattern.)

If this text were arranged alphabetically, what would the 13th word be?

The amount of women in London who flirt with their own husbands is perfectly scandalous. It looks so bad. It is simply washing one's clean linen in public.

Oscar Wilde

How many times can you read 878? The sequence is valid only if the numbers are joined by a line.

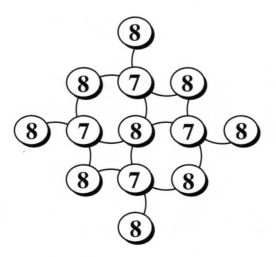

Words from a Richard Barnfield quote are scattered in the frame below. Following the arrows and using each word once, fill in the blanks to reveal the quote.

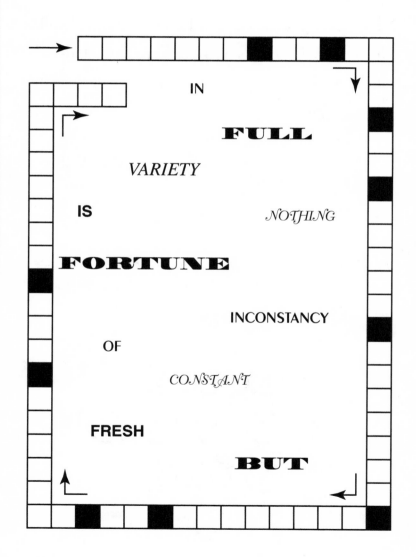

IN

FULL

VARIETY

IS

NOTHING

FORTUNE

INCONSTANCY

OF

CONSTANT

FRESH

BUT

Find seven different colors beginning with at least two of these letters.

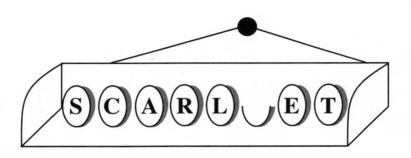

Add contiguous numbers (horizontally and vertically) so that they total 42. Each number may be used only once.

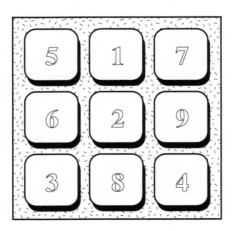

Follow the arrows as you fill in the blanks. Sum totals at arrows' ends must add up.

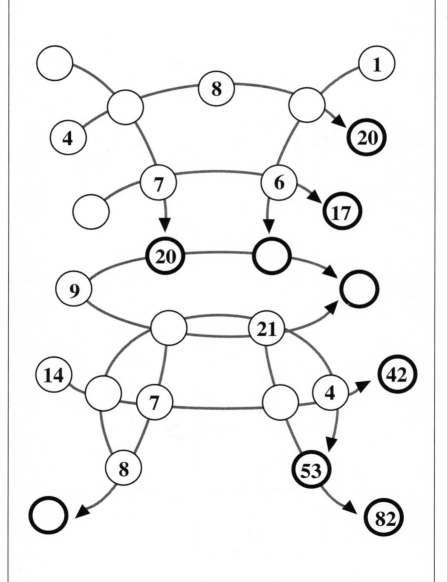

Find eight prime numbers on this grid. Each number is composed of a series of digits joined by line segments (or just one digit). Each digit may be used only once.

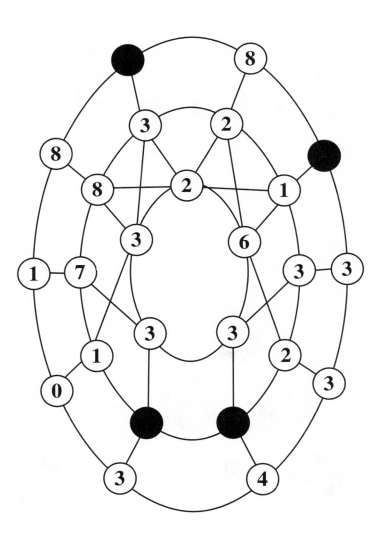

Can you find seven shorter words that compose the long one below? For example, *intergenerational* is made up of *in, gene, ratio, era, ration,* etc.

...fundamentally...

What is the missing number?

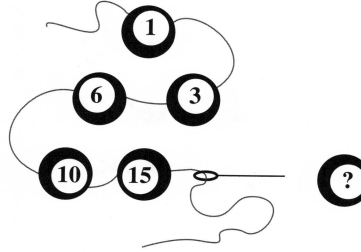

If the rectangles were placed one on top of another, what word would you be able to read?

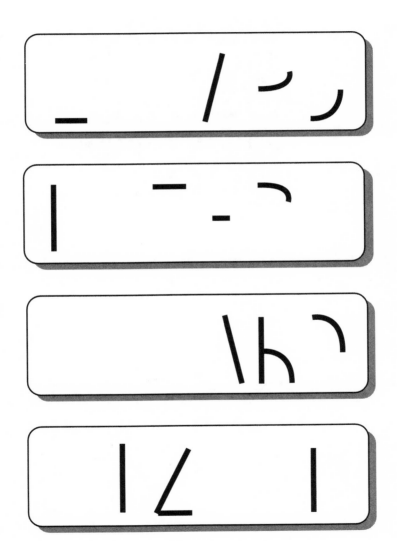

Most of the letters in this square are part of a logical pattern. However, one or more letters deviate from this pattern. Find the mistake.

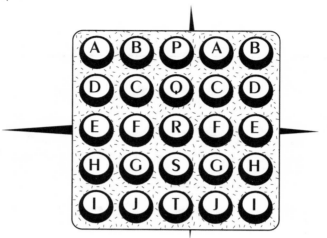

If the hexagons were placed one on top of another, what picture would you be able to see?

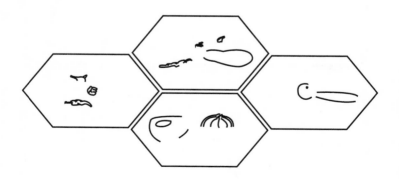

What is the logical relationship or pattern of the light-face numbers below? Which boldface number fits into this relationship (and thus should be lightface)?

1	2	3	4	**5**	6	**7**
8	**9**	**10**	**11**	12	**13**	14
15	**16**	**17**	18	**19**	20	**21**
22	**23**	24	**25**	**26**	**27**	**28**
29	30	**31**	**32**	**33**	**34**	**35**
36	**37**	38	**39**	**40**	**41**	42
43	44	**45**	**46**	**47**	**48**	**49**
50	**51**	**52**	**53**	54	**55**	**56**
57	**58**	**59**	60	**61**	62	**63**
64	**65**	**66**	**67**	68	**69**	**70**
71	72	**73**	74	**75**	**76**	**77**
78	**79**	80	**81**	**82**	**83**	84
85	**86**	**87**	**88**	**89**	90	**91**
92	**93**	**94**	**95**	**96**	**97**	98

Connect these ten numbers. Each number may be used only once and must have no divisor in common with the following one. Connecting lines may cross over each other.

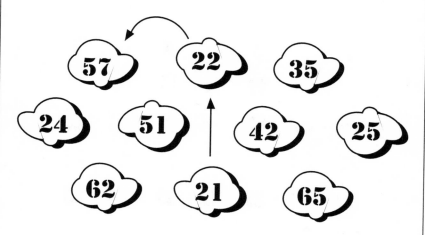

Fill in the blanks. The arrows indicate a common letter.

Bucket..............................

Chubby ....

Change...........................

Obvious.........................

If all the diagonals were removed, how many squares and rectangles would there be in this figure?

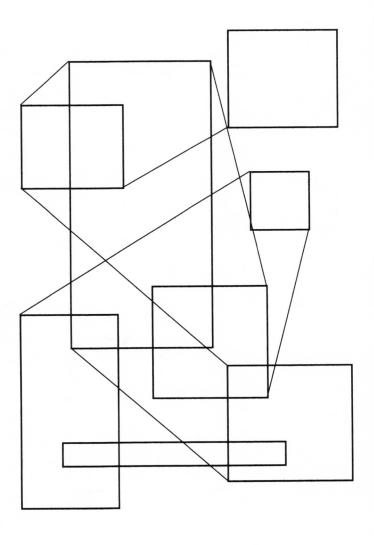

If the squares were circles, the circles were triangles, and the triangles were squares, how many

☐ circles would intersect a triangle?

☐ squares would be within a circle?

☐ triangles would enclose a square?

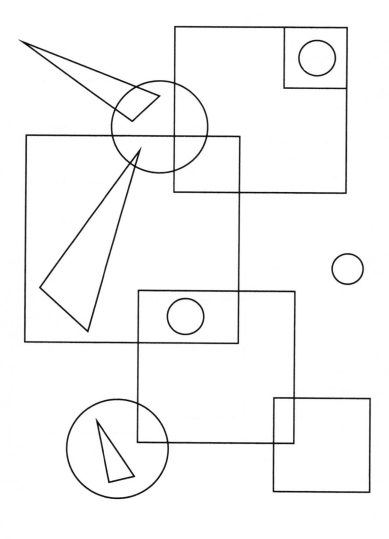

Fill in the blanks to find a William Blake quotation. The letters of the quotation are in alphabetical order in each column of the lower figure. Going from left to right, pick a letter from each column in the lower figure to compose the quote. Skip a column when figuring a space between words, and use each letter from each column once. Some lines of the quote break in the middle of words.

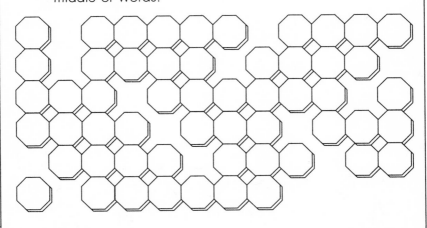

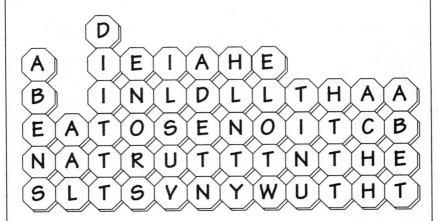

Using the A. J. Cronin quote directly below, decode the quote under it. Fill in the numbered blanks with the correct letters from Cronin's like-numbered words.

THEY   STOOD   LIKE   SOME   VAST   CHORUS,
1   2   3   4   5   6

MASSED   IN   SILENCE   AGAINST   THE
7   8   9   10   11

SNOW-DARK   SKY.
12   13   14

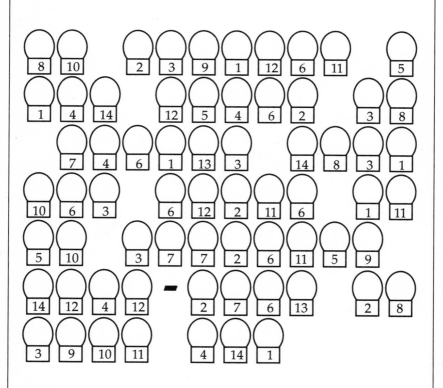

If the first square were turned upside down and placed on top of the second, you would be able to read the beginning of a sentence. After you have determined what that part of the sentence says, finish it by completing the math problem it contains.

	I		Λ	
	N		M	
ꓷN		Я		ꓷN
N		H O		⊥
O			Я O	
	ꓷ∩		ƎH⊥	

		S		A
R			O	T
F	W		U	
D		D A		
T	E		T	Y F
I	E	S		

Find the signs (+,−) that complete the equations.

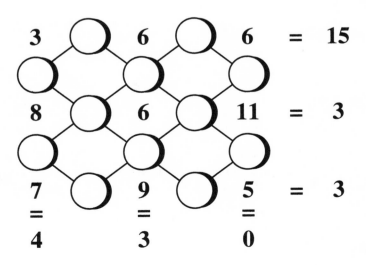

3 ◯ 6 ◯ 6 = 15

8 ◯ 6 ◯ 11 = 3

7 ◯ 9 ◯ 5 = 3

7 = 4   9 = 3   5 = 0

Add contiguous numbers (horizontally and vertically) so that they total 38. Each number may be used only once.

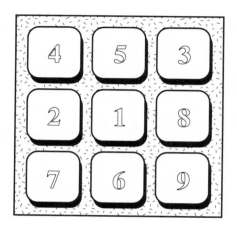

Find seven different authors beginning with at least two of these letters.

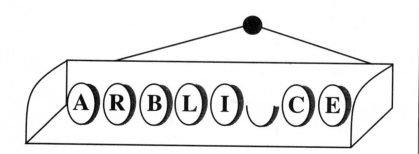

Words from a P. G. Wodehouse quote are scattered in the frame below. Following the arrows and using each word once, fill in the blanks to reveal the quote.

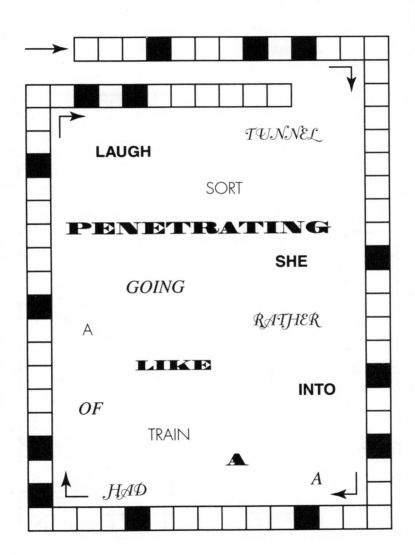

TUNNEL

LAUGH

SORT

PENETRATING

SHE

GOING

RATHER

A

LIKE

INTO

OF

TRAIN

A

HAD

A

Both grids contain the same words, spelled horizontally or vertically. If a word is spelled forward in one grid, it is spelled backward in the other, except for one word, which is spelled forward in both grids. Find all the words, and identify the exceptional word.

Y	P	T	R	U	H
X	E	M	I	L	K
A	N	E	N	I	W
L	I	C	P	T	W
A	C	A	I	E	I
G	I	R	L	A	N	T
Y	L	S	O	U	L	E	D
T	L	C	H	E	C	K	E	D
I	I	Y	O	G	H	U	R	T
L	N	B	B	E
I	T	A	R	M
B	O	N	U	A
A	M	J	G	G
T	B	L	I	A	N
P	C	O	F	F	E	E
E	D	R	A	W	E	R	S
C	G	C	I	R	C	U	S
C	B	A	L	L	P	U	B
A	S	I	L	L	E	R	T

T	R	E	L	L	I	S	A
I	S	U	C	R	I	C	C
S	R	E	W	A	R	D	C
T	R	U	H	G	O	Y	E
U	U	K	L	I	M	P
W	I	N	E	B	T
N	A	C	M	A
I	E	H	O	B
W	T	E	T	I
G	N	C	N	L
J	H	G	F	U	A	K	I	I
L	U	O	S	R	B	E	L	T
E	E	F	F	O	D	L	Y
H	U	R	T	G	I	G
Y	T	R	A	C	A
B	U	P	M	I	L
Y	T	R	E	N	A
N	A	I	L	E	X
L	L	A	B	P	Y

Fill in the blanks. Each side of the square is a logical sequence. The 2-headed arrows indicate a common number.

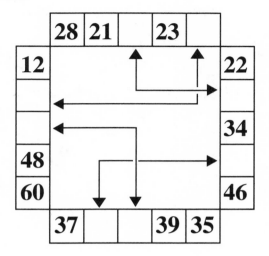

 Find seven different ways to resolve this problem.

You are happily driving along a country road on your motorcycle. Suddenly, you get a flat tire. What do you do?

How many times can you read 8808? The sequence is valid only if the numbers are joined by a line.

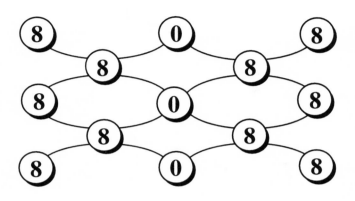

 If this text were arranged alphabetically, what would the 13th word be?

"Reeling and Writhing, of course, to begin with," the Mock Turtle replied; "and then the different branches of Arithmetic — Ambition, Distraction, Uglification, and Derision."

Lewis Carroll

Find seven different ways to make pairs with these words. (For example, *cow, calf, kid, cat: cow* and *calf* are the same species; *calf* and *kid* are the young of the species; *cat* and *calf* have the same first two letters.)

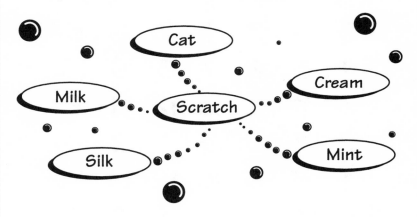

Using the listed items, devise a system that will logically determine the missing price.

Dessert

Apple Pie	8
Chocolate Cake	13
Ice Cream	8
Fruit Salad	?

Use a series of lines to join contiguous numbers whose sum equals 80. Start at "a" and finish at "b."

a

5 4 3 1 7 6 5

4 5 6 7 8 9 10

3 11 12 13 12 11 9

2 7 5 3 1 2 4

1 6 8 10 12 14 12

0 10 8 6 4 2 0

4 2 1 1 2 3 1

5 7 9 11 13 11 3

13 11 9 7 5 4 1

10 12 14 16 8 6 3

4 5 6 0 3 5 1

9 4 2 2 2 4 2

11 8 6 8 10 8 3

13 2 7 5 9 7 5

b

Follow the arrows as you fill in the blanks. Sum totals at arrows' ends must add up.

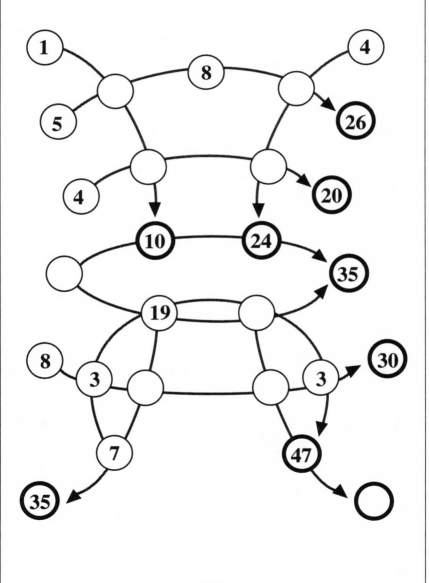

Find ten multiples of 7 on this grid. Each number is composed of a series of digits joined by line segments (or just one digit). Each digit may be used only once.

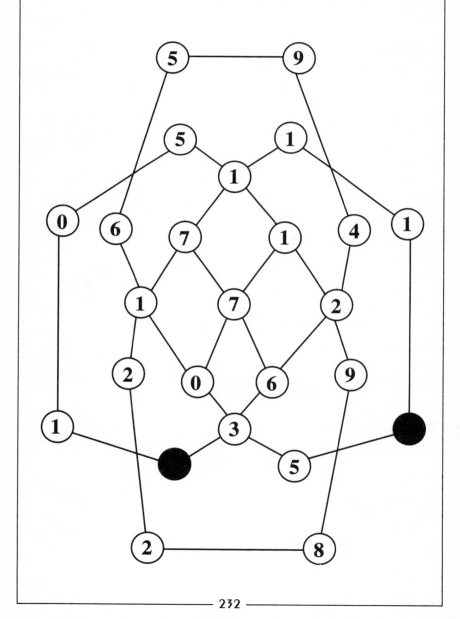

Complete the equation by filling in the five omissions with 1, 2, 3, 8, and 9. Each number may be used only once.

$$... + ... - (... \times ...) \div ... = 7$$

Find eleven synonyms of FOOLISH. Each word is written with horizontally and/or vertically connected letters. Each letter may be used only once.

S	D	D	L	U	D	I	C	R	O	U	S	H
E	I	I	G	F	N	O	N	S	E	N	S	I
N	N	D	I	O	T	D	A	F	T	I	S	C
S	J	U	Y	T	I	C	H	G	F	M	L	A
E	U	I	**F**	**O**	**O**	**L**	**I**	**S**	**H**	P	I	L
L	D	F	G	U	N	W	I	S	E	R	U	D
E	I	R	I	D	I	C	U	L	O	U	S	E
S	C	R	A	B	S	U	G	S	J	H	G	N
S	I	O	U	S	G	R	D	I	L	L	Y	T

Make seven longer words from *tin* by adding letters to it. For example, by adding letters to *hat*, you can get *t*hat, *hate*, *ch*at*ty*, *sh*at*ter*, *hatless*, *hatch*, etc.

...tin...

Fill in the blanks. Each line is a logical sequence. The arrows indicate a common number.

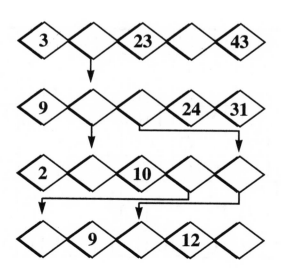

Complete this magic square so that it contains all of the numbers from 6 to 30. The sum of each line, column, and each of the two diagonals should be from 84 to 95.

9					**91**
					88
			25		**85**
	7		13		**94**
15	27			19	**92**
84					**90**
	89	**93**	**95**	**86**	**87**

Which instrument is distinct from the others?

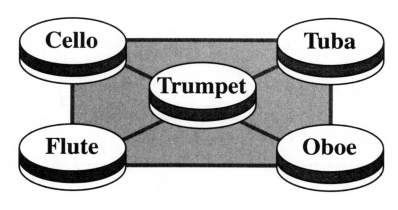

Cello   Tuba   Trumpet   Flute   Oboe

Make a word from the letters below, using each letter at least once. One letter must connect to another by a line in the diagram.

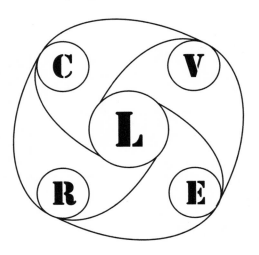

These numbers have many properties in common but do not share all the same traits. Find seven different reasons for determining what makes one or more of these numbers distinct from the rest.

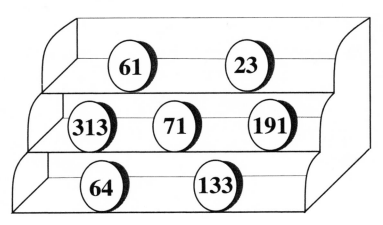

FISHERMEN

There are four fishermen in the port of Santa Helena: Andrew, Bertram, Charles, and David. Their boats are the Mary Jane, the Susan, the Seagull, and the Faithful. Unfortunately, the fishermen don't know one another quite as well as they think they do. You can only be sure what a fisherman says is true if his sentence contains information about his own boat. Otherwise, his affirmation is false.

> Andrew: "Other than my boat, the Susan and the Faithful are the only ones which have a radio."
>
> Bertram: "Charles is lucky to have one of the boats with a radio."
>
> Charles: "The Mary Jane is my boat."
>
> David: "I have been neither on the Faithful nor on the Mary Jane."

To whom does each boat belong?

If all the diagonals were removed, how many squares and rectangles would there be in this figure?

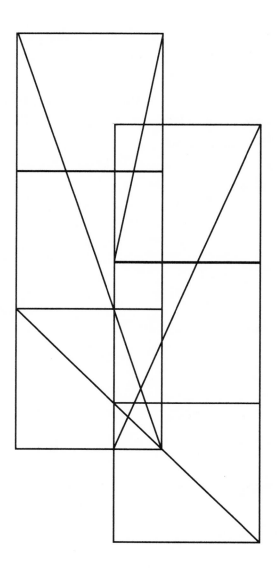

Fill in the blanks above the clue in italics. Then fill in the blanks of the frame, using those same letters. The 2-headed arrows indicate a common letter.

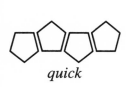

quick

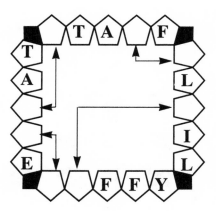

Replace each dot below with either 1, 3, 4, 5, 7, or 9 to make the problem add up correctly. Each number may be used only once.

```
    2 . . 1
 +  . . 7 6
 ───────────
    6 . 6 .
```

What is the logical relationship or pattern of the light-face numbers below? Which boldface number fits into this relationship (and thus should be lightface)?

1	**2**	69	**4**	**5**	**6**	**7**
8	**9**	**10**	**11**	**12**	**13**	**14**
60	**16**	**17**	**18**	**19**	**20**	**21**
22	**23**	**24**	**25**	51	**27**	**28**
29	49	**31**	**32**	**33**	**34**	**35**
36	**37**	**38**	78	**40**	**41**	**42**
43	**44**	**45**	**46**	**47**	**48**	30
50	26	**52**	**53**	**54**	**55**	**56**
57	**58**	**59**	15	**61**	**62**	**63**
64	**65**	**66**	**67**	**68**	3	**70**
71	**72**	96	**74**	**75**	**76**	**77**
39	**79**	**80**	**81**	**82**	**83**	**84**
85	**86**	**87**	**88**	**89**	**90**	**91**
92	**93**	**94**	**95**	73	**97**	**98**

These words and what they represent have many properties in common but do not share all the same traits. Find seven different reasons for determining what makes one or more of these words distinct from the rest.

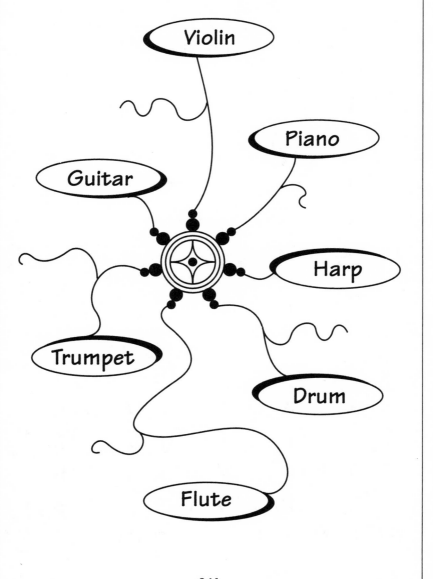

Fill in the blanks to find a Bernard Levin quotation. The letters of the quotation are in alphabetical order in each column of the lower figure. Going from left to right, pick a letter from each column in the lower figure to compose the quote. Skip a column when figuring a space between words, and use each letter from each column once. Some lines of the quote break in the middle of words.

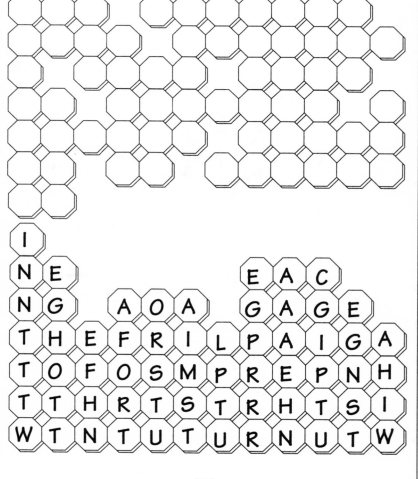

If the squares were circles, the circles were triangles, and the triangles were squares, how many

- [ ] circles would intersect a triangle?
- [ ] triangles would be within a circle?
- [ ] triangles would intersect a circle?

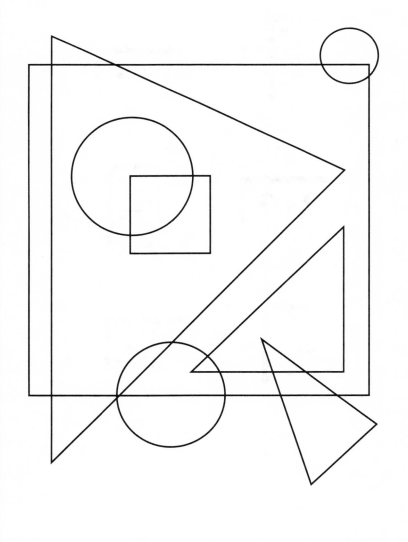

What is the numerical relationship of the dominoes below? Which domino is missing? (Their physical arrangement is not important.)

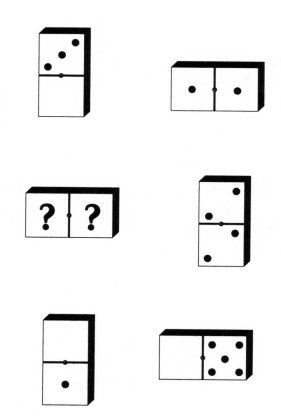

Find seven different trees beginning with at least two of these letters.

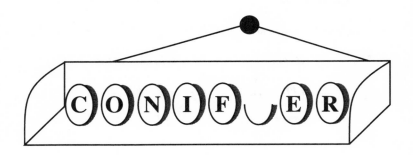

Add contiguous numbers (horizontally and vertically) so that they total 37. Each number may be used only once.

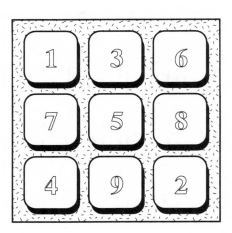

Make seven different sentences using only the words in this quote from John Keats.

I compare human life to a large mansion of many apartments, two of which I can only describe, the doors of the rest being as yet shut to me.

The figure on the left has ten weapons spelled forward or backward, in horizontally and/or vertically connected squares, but the figure on the right has only nine of these same weapons. Find all the weapons and identify the one missing on the right.

O	W	S	R	E	I	P	A	R	S		D	A	G	G
R	E	E	L	I	A	L	F	R	P		A	S	R	E
D	V	C	N	A	E	I	R	A	E		B	R	A	P
G	I	R	D	L	L	F					E	R	E	I
N	A	E	A				S	L	E	R	S	P	E	
I	L	G	G		R	G	G	N	I	L	F	I	R	A
L	G	S	A		E	E	D	R	O	W	S	C	N	R
S	R	E	B		I	V	L	I	A	L	F	E	A	L

What is the missing number?

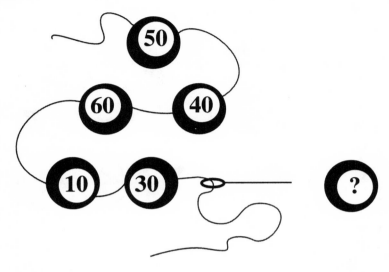

Can you find seven shorter words that compose the long one below? For example, *intergenerational* is made up of *in, gene, ratio, era, ration,* etc.

...hereinafter...

Words from a G. K. Chesterton quote are scattered in the frame below. Following the arrows and using each word once, fill in the blanks to reveal the quote.

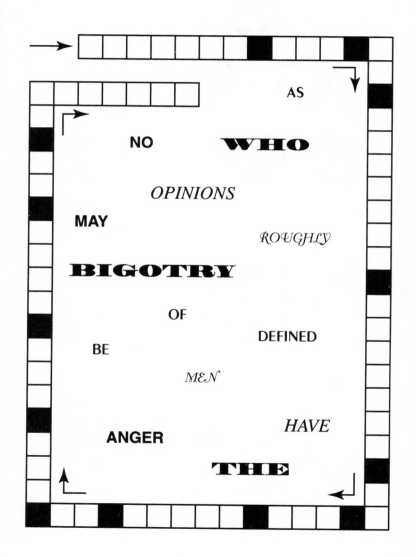

AS

NO   **WHO**

OPINIONS

MAY

ROUGHLY

BIGOTRY

OF

DEFINED

BE

MEN

HAVE

ANGER

THE

If the hexagons were placed one on top of another, what picture would you be able to see?

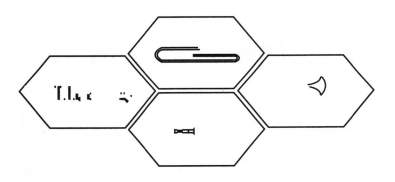

Most of the letters in this square are part of a logical pattern. However, one or more letters deviate from this pattern. Find the mistake.

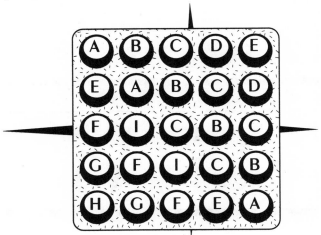

If the rectangles were placed one on top of another, what word would you be able to read?

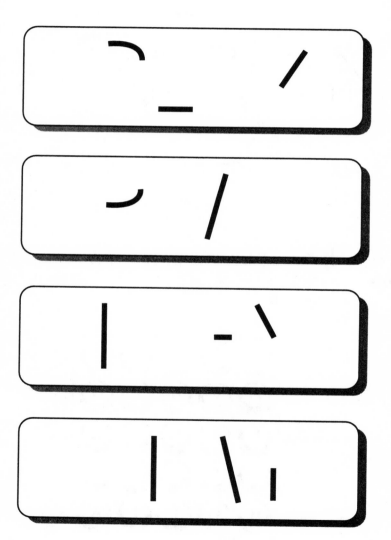

Fill in the blanks. The arrows indicate a common letter.

Movie ....

Pattern..

Dwarfed tree ....

Sure..................................

Connect these ten numbers. Each number may be used only once and must have no divisor in common with the following one. Connecting lines may cross over each other.

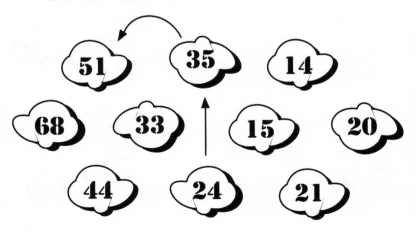

Follow the arrows as you fill in the blanks. Sum totals at arrows' ends must add up.

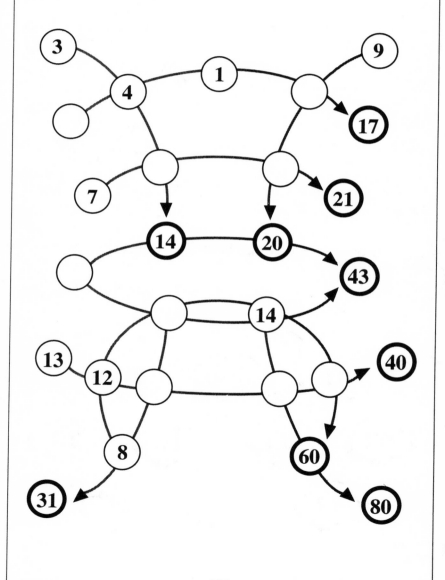

If this text were arranged alphabetically, what would the 13th word be?

Her own mother lived the latter years of her life in the horrible suspicion that electricity was dripping invisibly all over the house.

James Thurber

How many times can you read 612? The sequence is valid only if the numbers are joined by a line.

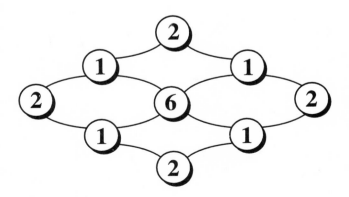

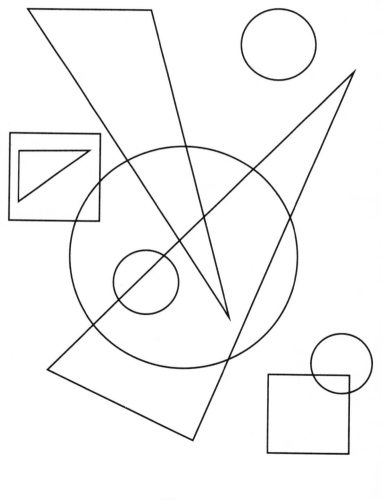

If the squares were triangles, the circles were squares,
and the triangles were circles, how many

☐ squares would intersect a circle?

☐ squares would intersect a triangle?

☐ triangles would enclose a circle?

If all the diagonals were removed, how many squares and rectangles would there be in this figure?

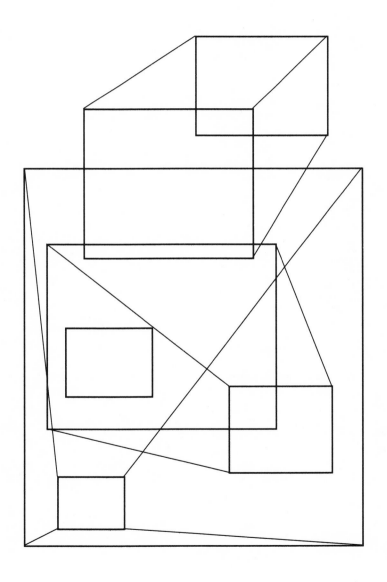

Find the signs (+,−) that complete the equations.

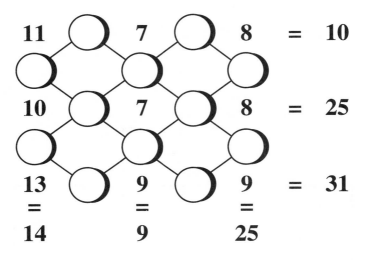

11 ◯ 7 ◯ 8 = 10
◯ ◯ ◯
10 ◯ 7 ◯ 8 = 25
◯ ◯ ◯
13 ◯ 9 ◯ 9 = 31
=   =   =
14   9   25

If the first square were turned upside down and placed on top of the second, you would be able to read the beginning of a sentence. After you have determined what that part of the sentence says, finish it by completing the math problem it contains.

Ǝ L I
O Ǝ
∀ Ǝ
S M N
Ǝ R H

T I T E
T I E T
H S Q U R
R O T O F
S X E N
I S

Using the Alexander Pope quote directly below, decode the quote under it. Fill in the numbered blanks with the correct letters from Pope's like-numbered words.

TRUE WIT IS NATURE TO ADVANTAGE DRESSED,
1   2   3   4   5   6   7

WHAT OFT WAS THOUGHT BUT NE'ER SO
8   9   10   11   12   13   14

WELL EXPRESSED.
15   16

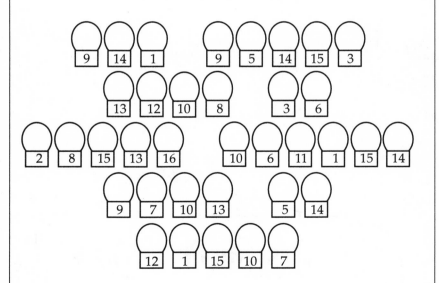

Add contiguous numbers (horizontally and vertically) so that they total 33. Each number may be used only once.

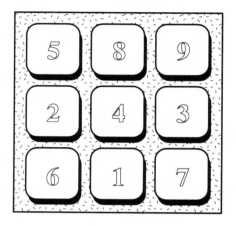

Find seven different flowers beginning with at least two of these letters.

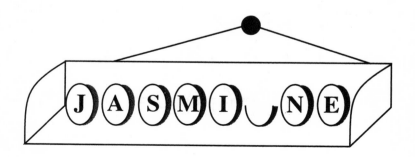

Find ten multiples of 3 on this grid. Each number is composed of a series of digits joined by line segments (or just one digit). Each digit may be used only once.

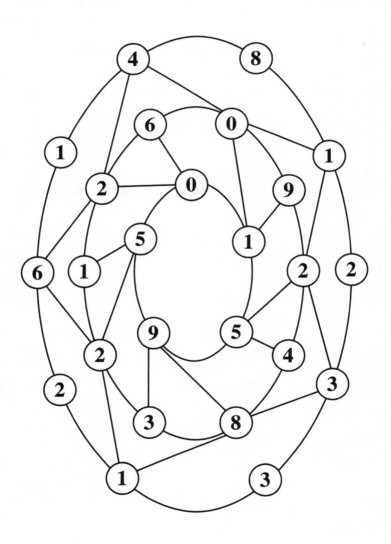

Using the listed items, devise a system that will logically determine the missing price.

Appetizers

Taramasalata	20
Avocado	22
Shrimp	19
Pâté	?

Find seven different ways to make pairs with these words. (For example, *cow, calf, kid, cat: cow* and *calf* are the same species; *calf* and *kid* are the young of the species; *cat* and *calf* have the same first two letters.)

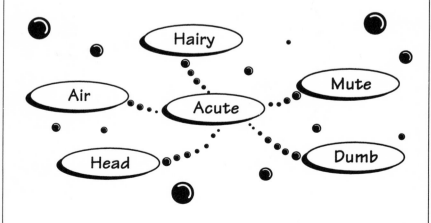

Hairy

Air

Acute

Mute

Head

Dumb

Both grids contain the same words, spelled horizontally or vertically. If a word is spelled forward in one grid, it is spelled backward in the other, except for one word, which is spelled forward in both grids. Find all the words, and identify the exceptional word.

C	H	A	R	M	L		S	S	E	N	Y	H	S	N
Y	T	U	A	E	B		E	M	O	T	I	O	N	O
G	K	I	N	D	E		Y	L	E	N	O	L	H	I
N	Y	T	S	E	Z		A	F	R	A	I	D	A	S
I	W	E	A	K	A			Z	E	S	T	Y	I	A
N	T	A	F	D	S	P		D	N	I	K	R	V	
N	C	D	G	I	I	A	R		B	A	D	Y	E	
U	I	A	N	U	O	N	J	G		M	R	A	H	C
C	M	I	O	G	N	O	U	T		G	U	I	L	T
Y	A	N	R	N						K	A	E	W	X
R	N	T	T	A		U	I	E	F	A	T	F	L	D
I	Y	Y	S	L		H	L	S	C	N	S	Y	A	Y
A	D	D	A	B		L	I	U	A	T	T	N	N	
H	H	A	P	P	Y		W	N	P	R	N	G	A	
S	H	Y	N	E	S	S		N	O	O	I	U	M	
W	L	L	O	N	E	L	Y		I	U	N	A	I	I
I	L	D	I	A	R	F	A		N	T	G	D	D	C
S	I	J	T	L	I	U	G		G	Y	P	P	A	H
E	N	O	I	T	O	M	E		B	E	A	U	T	Y

261

Find seven different ways to make pairs with these numbers.

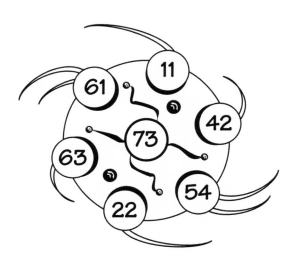

 Fill in the blanks. Each side of the square is a logical sequence. The arrows indicate a common number.

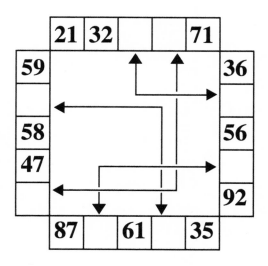

Fill in the blanks to find a Quentin Crisp quotation. The letters of the quotation are in alphabetical order in each column of the lower figure. Going from left to right, pick a letter from each column in the lower figure to compose the quote. Skip a column when figuring a space between words, and use each letter from each column once. Some lines of the quote break in the middle of words.

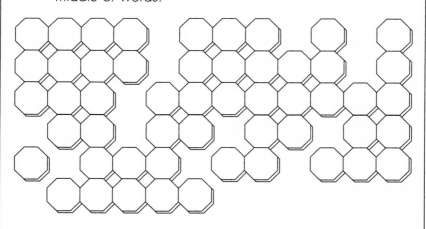

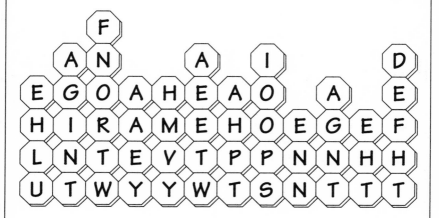

Find eleven synonyms of LOGICAL. Each word is written with horizontally and/or vertically connected letters. Each letter may be used only once.

R	Z	Z	C	F	R	E	L	E	P	E	R	T
E	A	F	O	H	E	G	V	V	A	N	T	I
G	S	J	G	F	R	O	B	V	I	O	U	N
V	O	U	L	L	E	N	T	H	G	F	S	E
A	N	D	**L**	**O**	**G**	**I**	**C**	**A**	**L**	I	N	N
L	A	I	S	O	U	R	A	T	I	O	N	T
I	B	C	I	J	N	G	C	W	I	S	A	J
D	L	G	O	D	D	G	O	H	G	E	L	L
H	E	G	U	S	F	D	G	E	N	T	U	Y

Complete the equation by filling in the five omissions with 1, 4, 5, 6, and 9. Each number may be used only once.

$$(\ldots + \ldots - \ldots) \times \ldots \div \ldots = 8$$

What is the logical relationship or pattern of the light-face numbers below? Which boldface number fits into this relationship (and thus should be lightface)?

1	**15**	**16**	17	**18**	**9**	**8**
7	2	**6**	5	**4**	3	17
16	**15**	3	**12**	11	**10**	**9**
10	11	**12**	**4**	3	2	1
9	**8**	7	**6**	5	7	**9**
11	13	**15**	17	**9**	**6**	**18**
17	3	**9**	2	**8**	**8**	7
2	**4**	**6**	**8**	**10**	**8**	**12**
14	**16**	**18**	17	**9**	7	5
3	1	**8**	**10**	**14**	2	**4**
6	**8**	11	**10**	**12**	**10**	1
3	**12**	5	**12**	**4**	7	**9**
13	**6**	**8**	**4**	13	11	**15**
11	**14**	13	1	**23**	**4**	1

Which bird is distinct from the others?

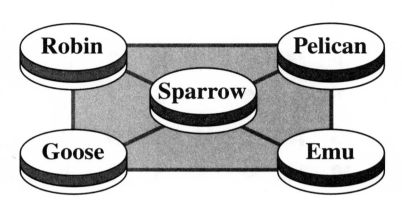

Complete this magic square so that it contains all of the numbers from 1 to 25. The sum of each line, column, and each of the two diagonals should be from 59 to 70.

	12		22		**67**
15			2		**69**
	20			1	**60**
	3	13	16		**63**
21		6		4	**66**
59				**65**	
	62	**61**	**70**	**68**	**64**

Words from a Dorothy Parker quote are scattered in the frame below. Following the arrows and using each word once, fill in the blanks to reveal the quote.

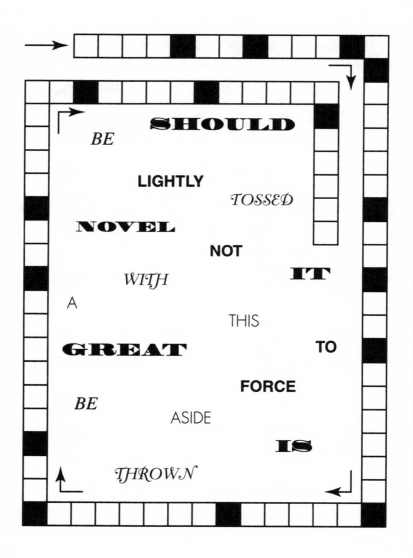

Hotels

Thomas has just returned from a trip abroad. He has made the following observations about foreign hotels and their restaurants:

> When the food is good, the waitresses are friendly.
>
> Year-round hotels have an ocean view.
>
> The food is bad only in certain cheap hotels.
>
> Hotels with a pool have honeysuckle climbing up their walls.
>
> Hotels with unfriendly waiters are open only for part of the year.
>
> Cheap hotels don't allow dogs.
>
> Hotels without a pool don't have an ocean view either.

In these places, can a dog owner smell the sweet odor of honeysuckle?

Use a series of lines to join contiguous numbers whose sum equals 270. Start at "a" and finish at "b."

a
1   2   3   5   7   9   11
3   2   10 12 13 14 15
4   16 17 9   11 20 18
9   17 16 10 4   1   19
19 20 21 22 5   30 31
32 29 28 27 10 26 27
8   9   10 14 20 15 16
17 18 17 18 15 14 13
1   3   2   8   5   6   7
1   25 31 9   4   7   9
10 11 12 13 4   14 15
16 17 18 8   4   20 21
22 12 19 3   6   9   10
28 29 30 4   1   5   8
b

How many times can you read 734? The sequence is valid only if the numbers are joined by a line.

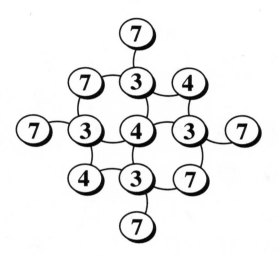

If this text were arranged alphabetically, what would the 13th word be?

I have heard of a man who had a mind to sell his house, and therefore carried a piece of brick in his pocket, which he showed as a pattern to encourage puchasers.

Jonathan Swift

Fill in the blanks. Each line is a logical sequence. The arrows indicate a common number.

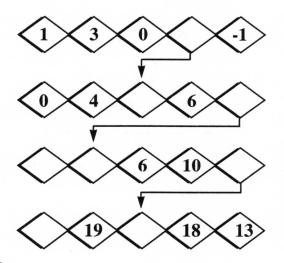

Make seven longer words from *ere* by adding letters to it. For example, by adding letters to *hat*, you can get **t**hat, hat**e**, **ch**at**ty**, **sh**at**ter**, hat**less**, hat**ch**, etc.

Replace each dot below with either 1, 3, 4, 5, or 8 to make the problem add up correctly. Each number may be used only once.

$$
\begin{array}{r}
9\ 7\ .\ 6\ \bullet \\
+\ \bullet\ 1\ .\ 5\ \bullet \\
\hline
1\ 1\ .\ 1\ \bullet
\end{array}
$$

Fill in the blanks above the clue in italics. Then fill in the blanks of the frame, using those same letters. The 2-headed arrows indicate a common letter.

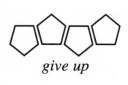

give up

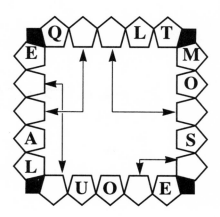

These numbers have many properties in common but do not share all the same traits. Find seven different reasons for determining what makes one or more of these numbers distinct from the rest.

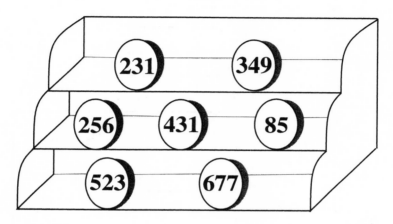

Make a word from the letters below, using each letter at least once. One letter must connect to another by a line in the diagram.

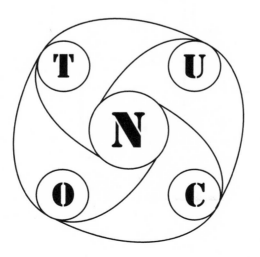

If all the diagonals were removed, how many squares and rectangles would there be in this figure?

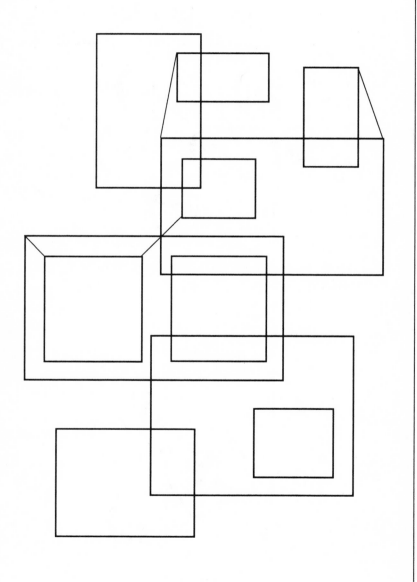

Follow the arrows as you fill in the blanks. Sum totals at arrows' ends must add up.

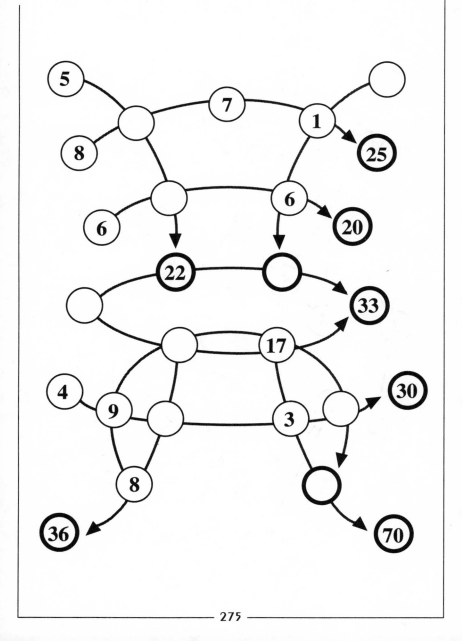

Find eleven square numbers on this grid. Each number is composed of a series of digits joined by line segments (or just one digit). Each digit may be used only once.

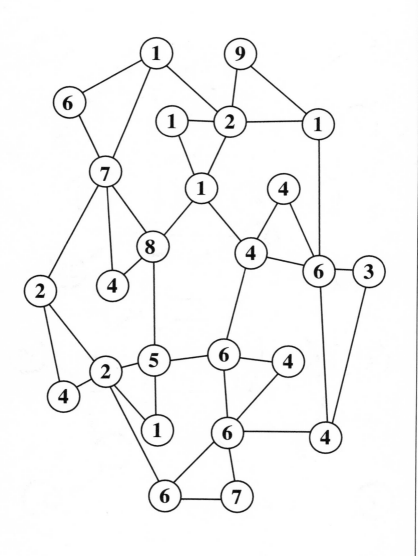

If the squares were circles, the circles were triangles, and the triangles were squares, how many

☐ circles would intersect a triangle?

☐ triangles would be within a square?

☐ triangles would intersect a square?

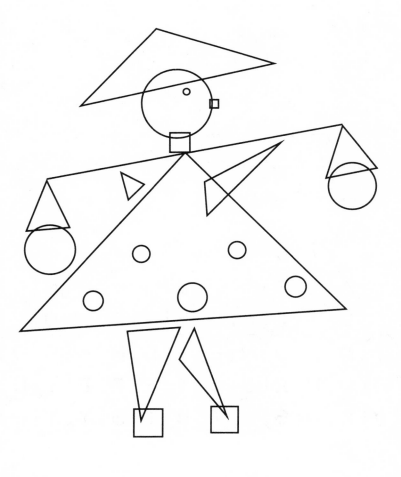

Fill in the blanks to find a Goodman Ace quotation. The letters of the quotation are in alphabetical order in each column of the lower figure. Going from left to right, pick a letter from each column in the lower figure to compose the quote. Skip a column when figuring a space between words, and use each letter from each column once. Some lines of the quote break in the middle of words.

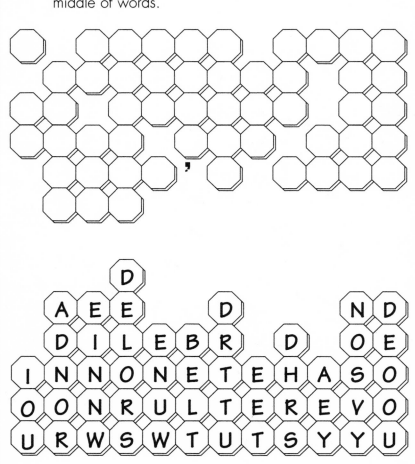

What is the numerical relationship of the dominoes below? Which domino is missing? (Their physical arrangement is not important.)

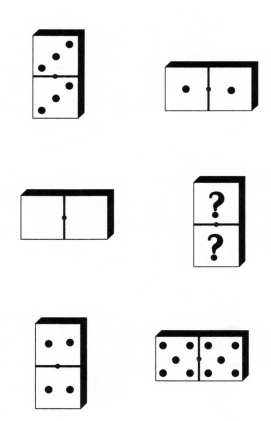

These words and what they represent have many properties in common but do not share all the same traits. Find seven different reasons for determining what makes one or more of these words distinct from the rest.

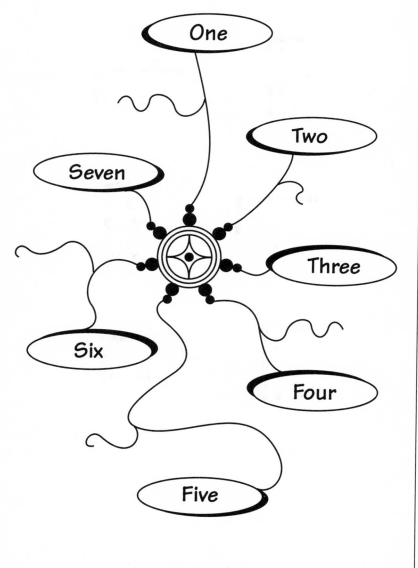

Find seven different musical instruments beginning with at least two of these letters.

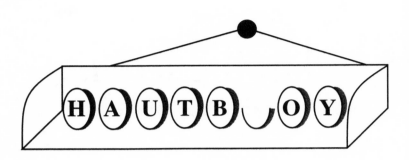

Add contiguous numbers (horizontally and vertically) so that they total 27. Each number may be used only once.

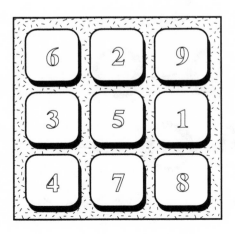

Can you find seven shorter words that compose the long one below? For example, *intergenerational* is made up of *in, gene, ratio, era, ration*, etc.

...kindhearted...

What is the missing number?

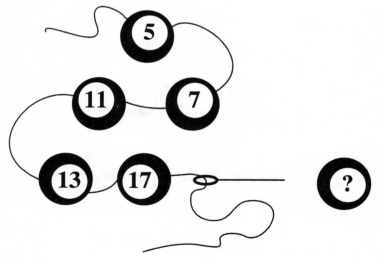

The figure on the left has ten countries spelled forward or backward, in horizontally and/or vertically connected squares, but the figure on the right has only nine of these same countries. Find all the countries and identify the one missing on the right.

E	R	U	N	R	B	R	A	Z	I		T	R	E	P
P	T	P	A	U	S	G	H	A	L		P	Y	G	E
F	P	A	G	A	S	I	A	N	A		T	A	G	E
R	Y	J	I	B	O	N					I	B	J	C
A	G	M	T				Y	L	A	T	O	A	N	
N	E	E	A		G	H	A	N	A	B	R	N	P	A
C	I	X	L		O	C	I	X	E	M	A	Z	A	R
E	C	O	Y		R	U	S	S	I	A	L	I	N	F

Make seven different sentences using only the words in this quote from William Congreve.

*He that first
cries out stop thief,
is often he that
has stolen the treasure.*

Most of the letters in this square are part of a logical pattern. However, one or more letters deviate from this pattern. Find the mistake.

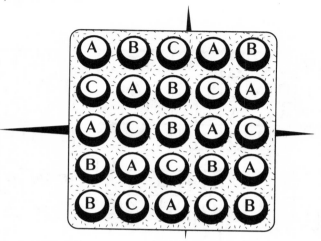

If the hexagons were placed one on top of another, what picture would you be able to see?

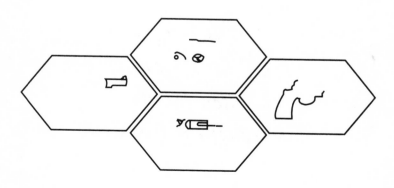

If the rectangles were placed one on top of another what word could you read?

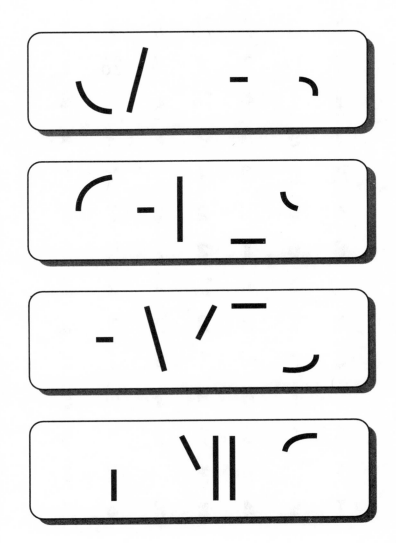

What is the logical relationship or pattern of the light-face numbers below? Which boldface number fits into this relationship (and thus should be lightface)?

8	3	2	75	5	7	1
0	12	8	2	5	26	7
1	6	0	25	4	5	4
1	9	9	2	5	3	4
12	0	5	1	3	62	1
4	9	31	6	8	7	5
8	0	1	2	7	18	3
99	3	6	19	2	4	6
3	2	0	8	18	2	66
4	6	47	1	5	7	3
0	1	5	9	7	17	8
6	2	3	7	8	9	9
1	14	6	2	74	0	1
7	9	4	8	5	0	22

If the first square were turned upside down and placed on top of the second, you would be able to read the beginning of a sentence. After you have determined what that part of the sentence says, finish it by completing the math problem it contains.

Find the signs (+,–) that complete the equations.

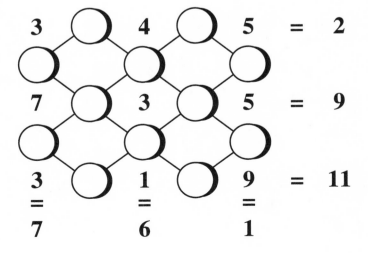

Fill in the blanks. The arrows indicate a common letter.

Quiet ....

Alas...

Enfeeble...

Tied ....

Connect these ten numbers. Each number may be used only once and must have no divisor in common with the following one. Connecting lines may cross over each other.

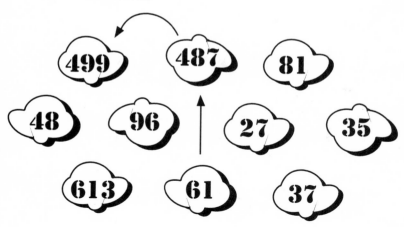

Fill in the blanks to find an Alain Jay quotation. The letters of the quotation are in alphabetical order in each column of the lower figure. Going from left to right, pick a letter from each column in the lower figure to compose the quote. Skip a column when figuring a space between words, and use each letter from each column once. Some lines of the quote break in the middle of words.

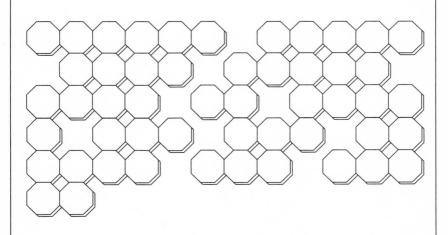

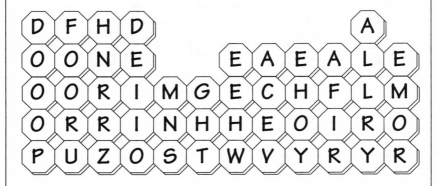

Using the William Dean Howells quote directly below, decode the William Cowper quote under it. Fill in the numbered blanks with the correct letters from Howells' like-numbered words.

SOME   PEOPLE   CAN   STAY   LONGER   IN
1   2   3   4   5   6

AN   HOUR   THAN   OTHERS   CAN   IN
7   8   9   10   11   12

A   WEEK.
13   14

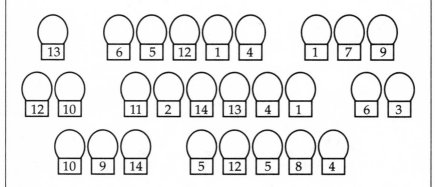

If this text were arranged alphabetically, what would the 13th word be?

No sooner met but they looked; no sooner looked but they loved; no sooner loved but they sighed; no sooner sighed but they asked one another the reason; no sooner knew the reason but they sought the remedy.

William Shakespeare

How many times can you read 52323? The sequence is valid only if the numbers are joined by a line.

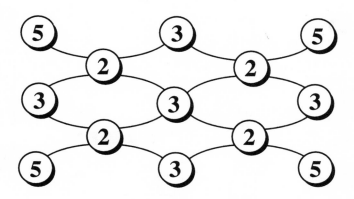

Words from a Winston Churchill quote are scattered in the frame below. Following the arrows and using each word once, fill in the blanks to reveal the quote.

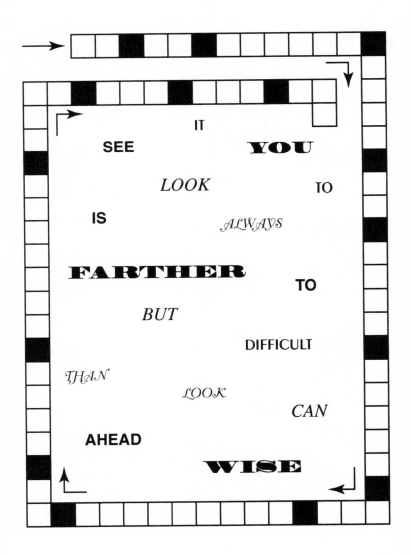

IT

SEE   YOU

LOOK   TO

IS   ALWAYS

FARTHER   TO

BUT

DIFFICULT

THAN   LOOK

CAN

AHEAD   WISE

If all the diagonals were removed, how many squares and rectangles would there be in this figure?

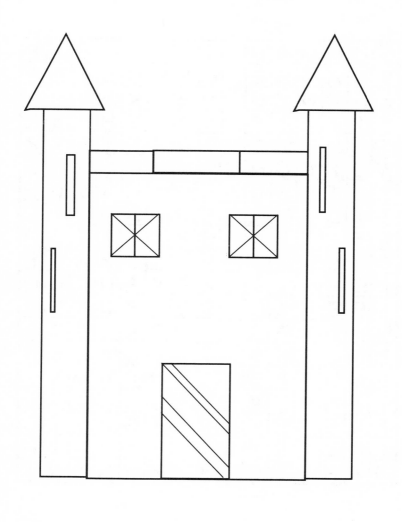

Both grids contain the same words, spelled horizontally or vertically. If a word is spelled forward in one grid, it is spelled backward in the other, except for one word. Find all the words, and identify the exceptional word.

S	U	M	M	O	N
E	P	A	C	S	E
R	N	P	N	V	G
A	I	I	I	I	E
T	P	D	T	M	P
W	E	L	C	O	M	E
R	E	T	H	G	U	A	L
I	T	G	C	U	R	V	E	D
N	S	L	T	E	K	C	O	P
C	U	O	W	X
L	G	V	I	L
I	S	E	N	I
N	I	H	E	A
E	D	G	F	N	B
D	S	U	F	F	E	R
T	T	N	A	V	R	E	S
P	R	E	T	E	N	D	D
I	N	V	E	R	T	E	D
G	T	N	E	L	O	I	V

V	I	O	L	E	N	T	F
G	E	M	O	C	L	E	W
D	E	T	R	E	V	N	I
L	A	U	G	H	T	E	R
	D	N	E	T	E	R	P
	N	O	M	M	U	S
	N	J	E	D	E
	A	D	N	I	V
	I	I	I	S	O
	L	P	W	G	L
S	E	R	V	A	N	T	U	G
H	D	E	V	R	U	C	S	D
P	O	C	K	E	T	T	E
E	S	C	A	P	E	N
U	P	U	M	K	I
J	E	G	I	K	L
T	G	P	V	T	C
A	I	I	N	I	N
R	G	N	Y	N	I

Find nine multiples of 11 on this grid. Each number is composed of a series of digits joined by line segments (or just one digit). Each digit may be used only once.

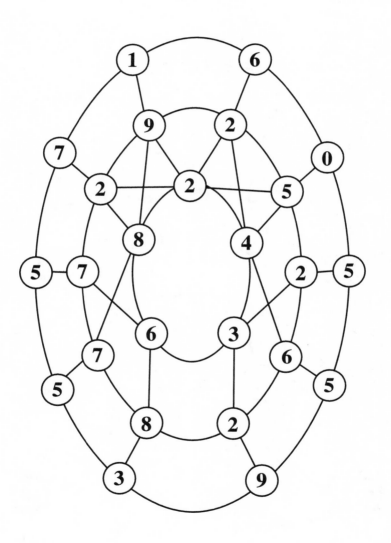

Follow the arrows as you fill in the blanks. Sum totals at arrows' ends must add up.

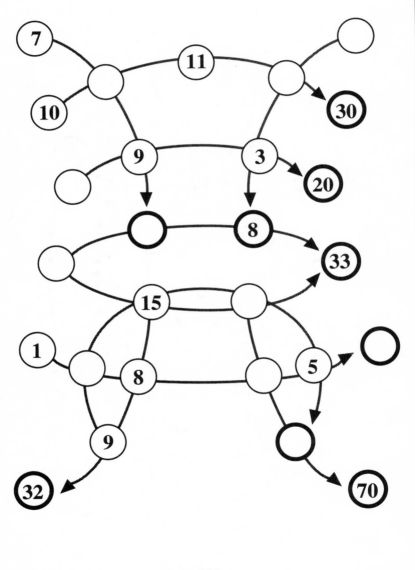

Using the listed items, devise a system that will logically determine the missing price.

Cocktails

Whisky 11.50

Tequila 10.00

Vodka 11.00

House Cocktail .... ?

Find seven different ways to make pairs with these words. (For example, *cow, calf, kid, cat: cow* and *calf* are the same species; *calf* and *kid* are the young of the species; *cat* and *calf* have the same first two letters.)

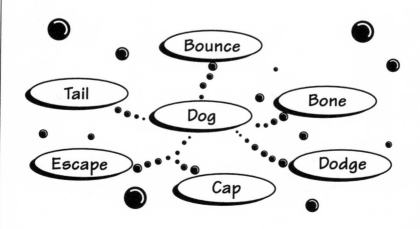

If the squares were triangles, the circles were squares, and the triangles were circles, how many

☐ circles would intersect a triangle?

☐ triangles would be within a square?

☐ squares would intersect a circle?

What is the logical relationship or pattern of the light-face numbers below? Which boldface number fits into this relationship (and thus should be lightface)?

1	**2**	**3**	**4**	**5**	**6**	7
26	**25**	**24**	**23**	**22**	21	**8**
27	**39**	**40**	**41**	42	**43**	**9**
28	**44**	**45**	**46**	**47**	**48**	**10**
29	**49**	**50**	**51**	**52**	**53**	**11**
30	**54**	**55**	56	**57**	**58**	**12**
31	**59**	**60**	**61**	**62**	63	**13**
32	**64**	**65**	**66**	**67**	**68**	14
33	**69**	70	**71**	**72**	**73**	**15**
34	**74**	**75**	**76**	77	**78**	**16**
35	**79**	**80**	**81**	**82**	**83**	**17**
36	84	**85**	**86**	**87**	**88**	**18**
37	**89**	**90**	91	**92**	**93**	**19**
38	**94**	**95**	**96**	**97**	98	**20**

Add contiguous numbers (horizontally and vertically) so that they total 28. Each number may be used only once.

Find seven different items of clothing beginning with at least two of these letters.

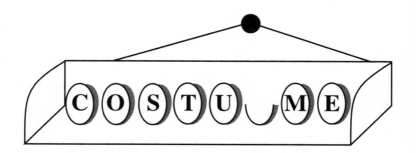

Complete the equation by filling in the five omissions with 1, 2, 6, 7, and 8. Each number may be used only once.

$$(\ldots + \ldots - \ldots) \times \ldots \div \ldots = 3$$

Find eleven synonyms of CONCEAL. Each word is written with horizontally and/or vertically connected letters. Each letter may be used only once.

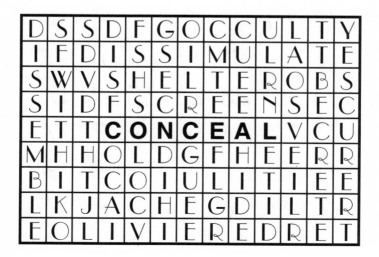

D	S	S	D	F	G	O	C	C	U	L	T	Y
I	F	D	I	S	S	I	M	U	L	A	T	E
S	W	V	S	H	E	L	T	E	R	O	B	S
S	I	D	F	S	C	R	E	E	N	S	E	C
E	T	T	**C**	**O**	**N**	**C**	**E**	**A**	**L**	V	C	U
M	H	H	O	L	D	G	F	H	E	E	R	R
B	I	T	C	O	I	U	L	I	T	I	E	E
L	K	J	A	C	H	E	G	D	I	L	T	R
E	O	L	I	V	I	E	R	E	D	R	E	T

Use a series of lines to join contiguous numbers whose sum equals 300. Start at "a" and finish at "b."

a

1	2	4	6	8	10	12
14	16	12	8	6	9	13
17	13	11	10	12	10	8
19	21	23	24	25	26	27
21	16	30	31	32	33	8
9	2	3	4	9	2	10
7	6	5	4	3	2	11
18	17	16	15	14	13	12
11	10	2	2	1	5	7
9	8	21	17	18	19	20
21	22	23	25	27	29	31
32	34	36	35	3	5	7
5	3	1	7	2	8	9
7	9	1	7	6	5	10

b

Complete this magic square so that it contains all of the numbers from 1 to 25. The sum of each line, column, and each of the two diagonals should be from 59 to 70.

		13	7	3	**63**
17			21		**66**
11	1	23		20	**60**
22		9			**67**
	25	19		8	**69**

59   **65**

68	**64**	**70**	**62**	**61**

Which boat is distinct from the others?

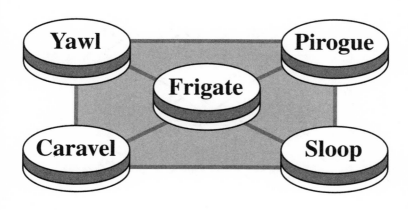

Yawl   Pirogue   Frigate   Caravel   Sloop

Make seven longer words from *key* by adding letters to it. For example, by adding letters to *hat*, you can get **t**hat, hat**e**, **c**hat**ty**, **s**hat**ter**, hat**less**, hat**ch**, etc.

...key...

Fill in the blanks. Each line is a logical sequence. The arrows indicate a common number.

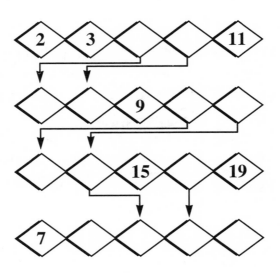

Replace each dot below with 1, 2, 3, 4, or 9 to make the problem add up correctly. Each number may be used only once.

$$
\begin{array}{r}
5\ .\ .\ 1 \\
+\ 6\ 8\ 0\ . \\
\hline
1\ .\ .\ 9\ 5
\end{array}
$$

Fill in the blanks above the clue in italics. Then fill in the blanks of the frame, using those same letters. The 2-headed arrows indicate a common letter.

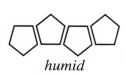

humid

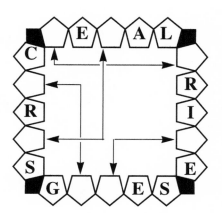

These numbers have many properties in common but do not share all the same traits. Find seven different reasons for determining what makes one or more of these numbers distinct from the rest.

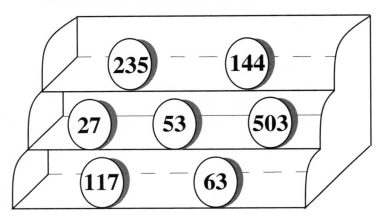

Make a word from the letters below, using each letter at least once. One letter must connect to another by a line in the diagram.

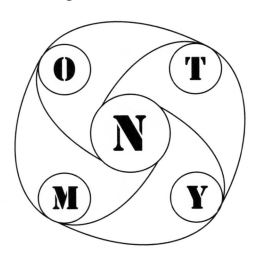

Words from a Tennessee Williams quote are scattered in the frame below. Following the arrows and using each word once, fill in the blanks to reveal the quote.

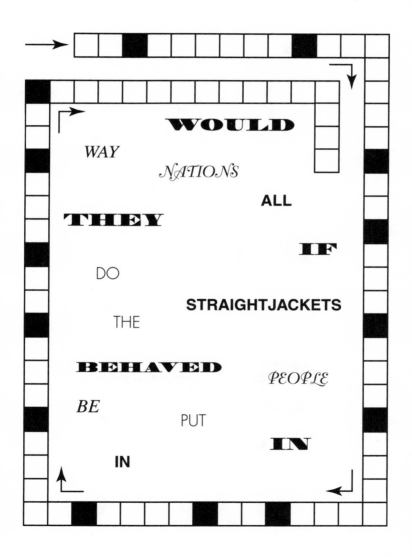

WOULD

WAY

NATIONS

ALL

THEY

IF

DO

STRAIGHTJACKETS

THE

BEHAVED

PEOPLE

BE

PUT

IN

IN

What is the numerical relationship of the dominoes below? Which domino is missing? (Their physical arrangement is not important.)

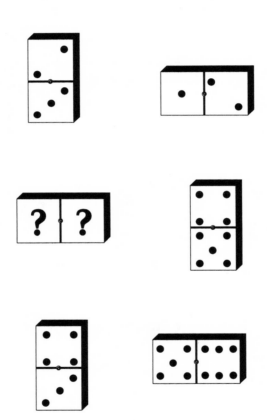

Holdup

After a holdup, four bank employees try to give a description of the thief.

According to the receptionist, he was tall, had blue eyes, and wore a jacket and a hat.

According to the teller, his eyes were black, he was small, and he was wearing a jacket and a hat.

According to the secretary, he was of medium height, had green eyes, and wore a raincoat and a hat.

According to the manager, his eyes were gray, he was small, and he was wearing a jacket but no hat.

Each witness has remembered only one detail out of four correctly. Furthermore, each detail was described correctly by at least one witness.

What is the exact description of the thief?

Fill in the blanks to find a Thomas Campbell quotation. The letters of the quotation are in alphabetical order in each column of the lower figure. Going from left to right, pick a letter from each column in the lower figure to compose the quote. Skip a column when figuring a space between words, and use each letter from each column once. Some lines of the quote break in the middle of words.

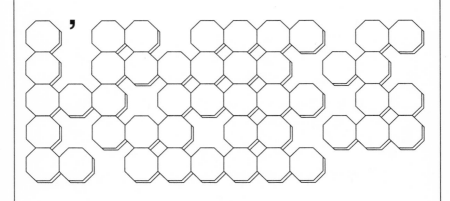

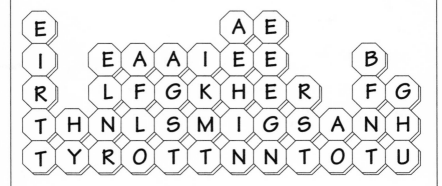

These words and what they represent have many properties in common but do not share all the same traits. Find seven different reasons for determining what makes one or more of these words distinct from the rest.

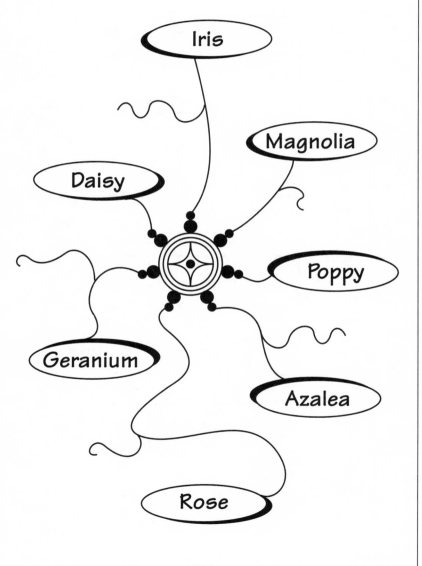

If all the diagonals were removed, how many squares and rectangles would there be in this figure?

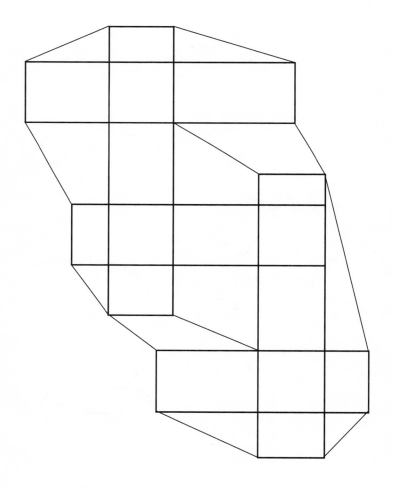

What is the missing number?

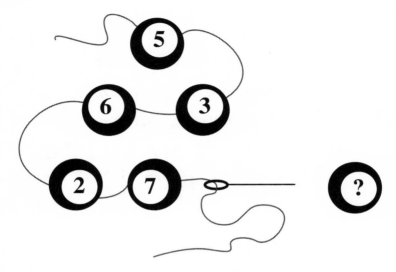

 Can you find seven shorter words that compose the long one below? For example, *intergenerational* is made up of *in, gene, ratio, era, ration*, etc.

...participate...

Make seven different sentences using only the words in this quote from William Cowper.

With outstretched hoe
I slew him at the door,
And taught him
NEVER TO COME THERE
NO MORE.

The figure on the left has twelve lakes spelled forward or backward, in horizontally and/or vertically connected squares, but the figure on the right has only eleven of these same lakes. Find all the lakes and identify the one missing on the right.

H	E	R	Y	G	I	H	C	I	M		O	N	E	T
R	N	O	E	A	N	H	U	R	O		M	O	R	E
A	D	O	M	B	I	L	U	H	N		O	E	Y	M
O	M	C	O	A	W	A					C	D	A	E
L	E	A	D				H	U	L	A	D	A	O	
E	M	A	N		C	H	H	U	R	O	N	W	I	B
D	A	H	C		I	I	N	I	R	A	H	A	L	O
E	I	R	E		M	G	A	E	E	D	C	M	E	N

If the hexagons were placed one on top of another, what picture would you be able to see?

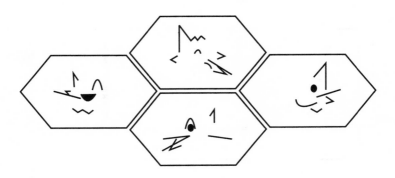

Most of the letters in this square are part of a logical pattern. However, one or more letters deviate from this pattern. Find the mistake.

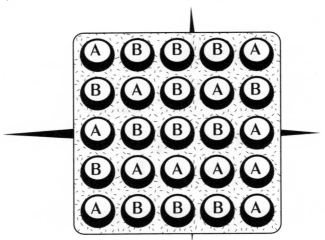

If the rectangles were placed one on top of another, what word would you be able to read?

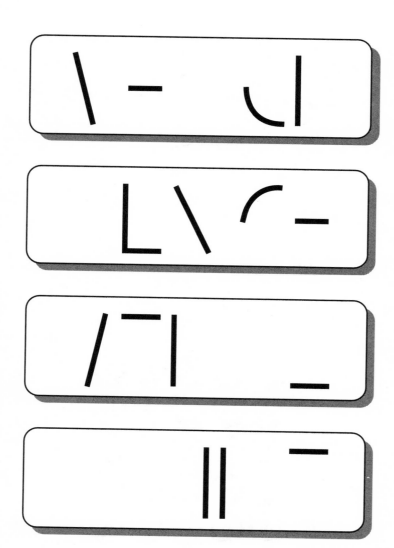

Connect these ten numbers. Each number may only be used once and must have no divisor in common with the following one. Connecting lines may cross over each other.

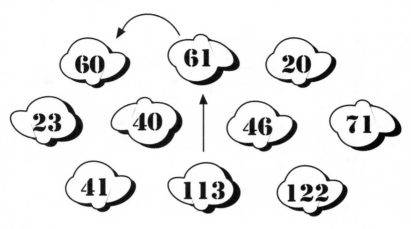

Fill in the blanks. The arrows indicate a common letter.

3600 seconds ....

Push ....

Study ....

Ripple ....

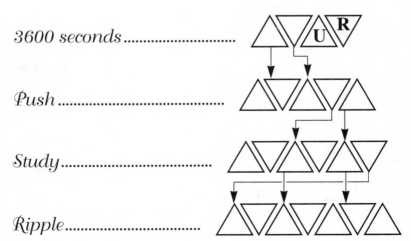

Find the signs (+,−) that complete the equations.

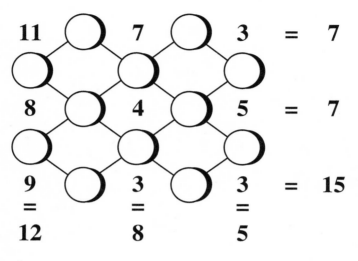

11 ◯ 7 ◯ 3 = 7

8 ◯ 4 ◯ 5 = 7

9 ◯ 3 ◯ 3 = 15

9 = 12   3 = 8   3 = 5

If the first square were turned upside down and placed on top of the second, you would be able to read the beginning of a sentence. After you have determined what that part of the sentence says, finish it by completing the math problem it contains.

```
              I
    Ǝ      ∩
      Я  O
  Ⅎ  S  I
    Ⅎ
    ⊥  O  ∩
      Я      H
```

```
T    E  P      O  D
   C  T      F      H
E  F      R      T
   U      P      I  M
E  N      M  B      R
S      S
```

Using the William Shakespeare quote directly below, decode the Francis Bacon quote under it. Fill in the numbered blanks with the correct letters from Shakespeare's like-numbered words.

BEAUTY   PROVOKETH   THIEVES
1   2   3

SOONER   THAN   GOLD.
4   5   6

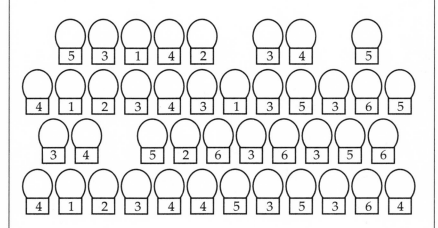

How many times can you read 1161? The sequence is valid only if the numbers are joined by a line.

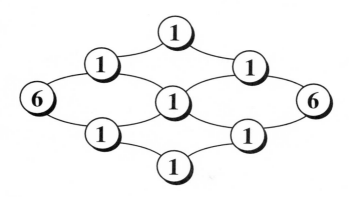

If this text were arranged alphabetically, what would the 13th word be?

A fool with judges, amongst fools a judge:
He says but little, and that little said
Owes all its weight, like loaded dice, to lead.
His wit invites you by his looks to come,
But when you knock, it never is at home.

William Cowper

Fill in the blanks. Each side of the square is a logical sequence. The arrows indicate a common number.

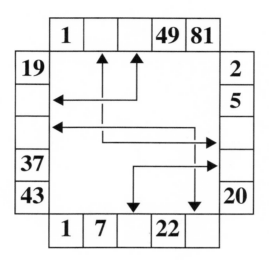

Find seven different ways to make pairs with these numbers.

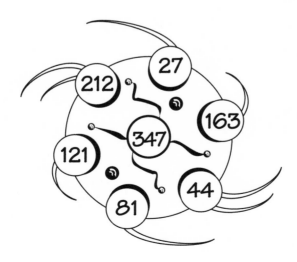

Find ten square numbers on this grid. Each number is composed of a series of digits joined by line segments (or just one digit). Each digit may be used only once.

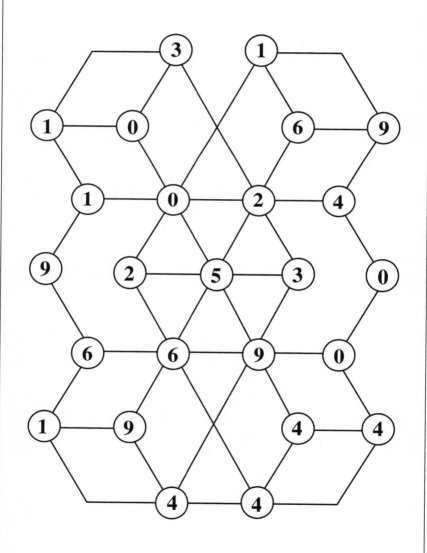

Follow the arrows as you fill in the blanks. Sum totals at arrows' ends must add up.

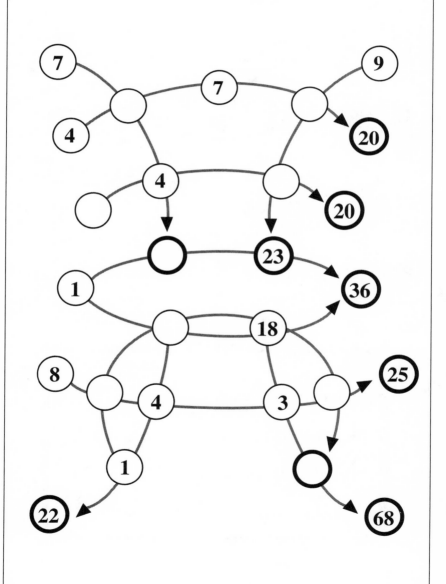

Find seven different ways to make pairs with these words. (For example, *cow, calf, kid, cat: cow* and *calf* are the same species; *calf* and *kid* are the young of the species; *cat* and *calf* have the same first two letters.)

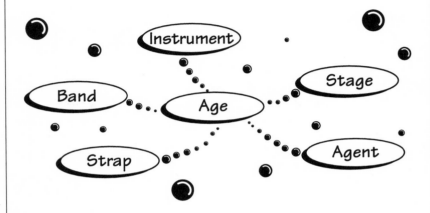

Using the listed items, devise a system that will logically determine the missing price.

Drinks

Tea 6

Coffee 12

Milk 8

Soda .... ?

Both grids contain the same words, spelled horizontally or vertically. If a word is spelled forward in one grid, it is spelled backward in the other. Find all the words.

N	C	O	I	N	C		T	E	N	S	I	O	N	N
O	C	I	N	O	I		N	O	I	H	S	U	C	O
I	B	N	I	A	M		F	I	C	T	I	O	N	I
T	P	A	I	N	G		N	O	I	T	A	V	O	L
A	N	O	I	C	S		C	A	P	T	I	O	N	N
S	A	C	T	I	O	N	H	R	O	A	J	I
N	N	O	I	T	P	A	C	A	N	U	N	O
E	E	N	O	I	T	C	I	F	D	A	D	O	N
S	M	O	V	A	T	I	O	N	I	I	I	I	I
O	O	O	L	P		O	P	O	T	C
I	T	I	I	I	N	O	I	S	S	I	M	O	S
D	I	D	O	A	V	E	R	S	I	O	N	M	E
A	O	U	T	N	M	N	I	K	S	V	E	N
R	N	A	W	O	J	N	O	I	T	C	A	S
N	O	I	S	N	E	T	T	M	A	I	N	A
C	U	S	H	I	O	N	L	O	B	I	N	Z	T
S	K	I	N	N	I	B	I	I	N	I	A	P	I
N	O	I	S	R	E	V	O	L	N	I	O	C	O
M	I	S	S	I	O	N	N	S	C	I	O	N	N

The arrows show the first two crabs in a sequence that is determined by some physical attribute(s) of the crabs. Provide the reasoning that allows the rest of the crabs to be joined in this sequence. Then give the full sequence by number. (In some cases, there may be more than one sequence that satisfies the pattern.)

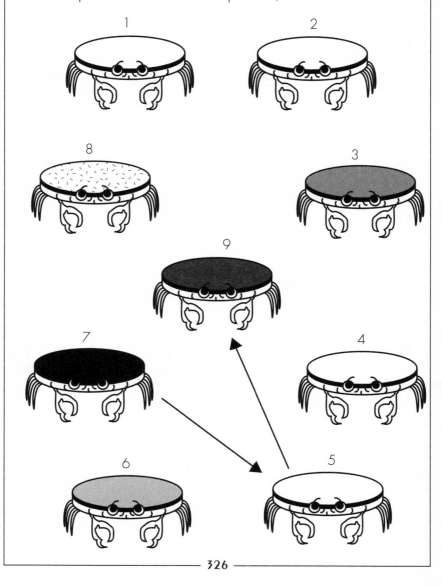

If the squares were circles, the circles were triangles, and the triangles were squares, how many

[ ] circles would intersect a triangle?

[ ] squares would be within a circle?

[ ] triangles would enclose a square?

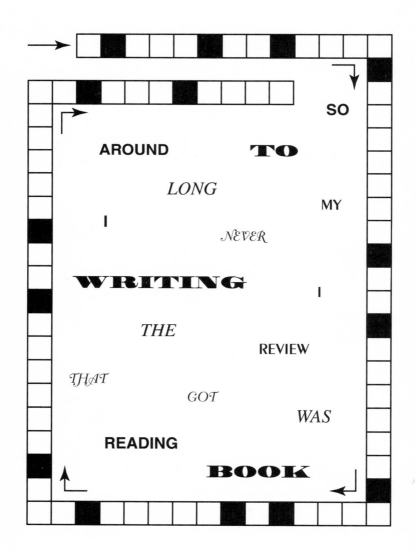

Words from a Groucho Marx quote are scattered in the frame below. Following the arrows and using each word once, fill in the blanks to reveal the quote.

SO

AROUND   TO

LONG

MY

I

NEVER

WRITING

I

THE

REVIEW

THAT

GOT

WAS

READING

BOOK

Insert +, −, x, and/or parentheses between the numbers to find the total.

1 2 3 4 5 6 7 8 9

=

62

Connect these twelve cities. Each city may be used only once and must have no letters in common with the following one. Connecting lines may cross over each other.

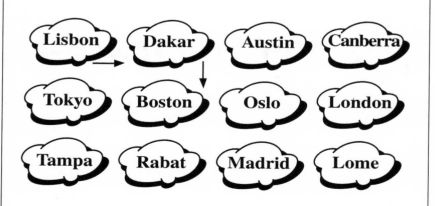

Lisbon Dakar Austin Canberra

Tokyo Boston Oslo London

Tampa Rabat Madrid Lome

Find nine synonyms of PLACATE. Each word is written with horizontally and/or vertically connected letters. Each letter may be used only once.

A	S	S	K	M	O	L	L	I	F	Y	H	H
P	L	O	O	T	G	P	A	C	C	O	N	C
P	O	I	U	H	E	F	D	I	K	S	D	I
E	A	S	E	F	G	H	J	F	Y	A	Z	L
J	H	G	**P**	**L**	**A**	**C**	**A**	**T**	**E**	T	Y	I
G	U	J	H	G	C	A	L	M	U	I	S	A
H	M	H	A	S	S	E	R	T	Y	S	D	T
J	O	L	K	L	U	G	H	J	K	F	G	E
V	R	E	A	S	A	G	E	U	I	Y	O	I

 Complete the equation by filling in the five omissions with 2, 3, 7, 8, and 9. Each number may be used only once.

$$[... + ... - (... \times ...)] \div ... = 1$$

If all the diagonals were removed, how many squares and rectangles would there be in this figure?

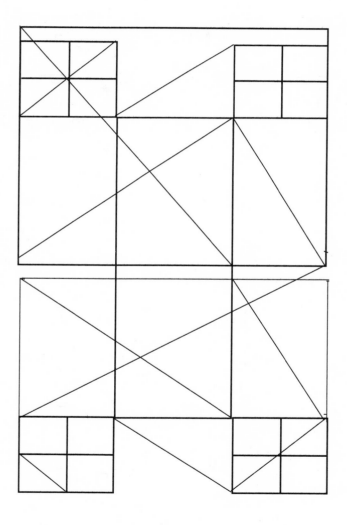

Which color is distinct from the others?

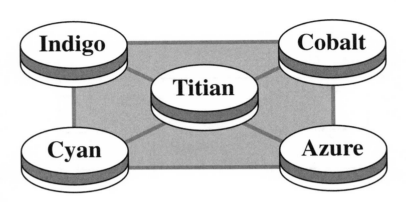

 Complete this magic square so that it contains all of the numbers from 1 to 25. The sum of each line, column, and each of the two diagonals should be 65.

	16	25			65
20		7		24	65
21			17	5	65
	15		23		65
14		1			65

65				65

65	65	65	65	65

Fill in the blanks to find an Aldous Huxley quotation. The letters of the quotation are in alphabetical order in each column of the lower figure. Going from left to right, pick a letter from each column in the lower figure to compose the quote. Skip a column when figuring a space between words, and use each letter from each column once. Some lines of the quote break in the middle of words.

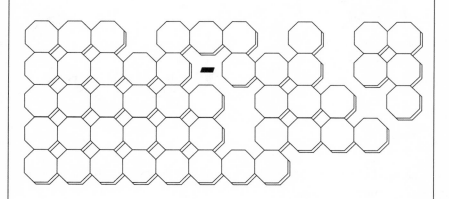

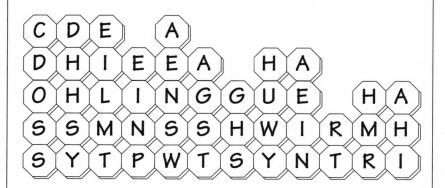

Fill in the blanks above the clue in italics. Then fill in the blanks of the frame, using those same letters. The 2-headed arrows indicate a common letter.

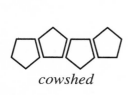

cowshed

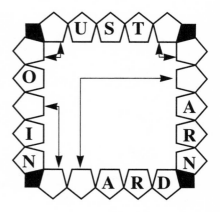

Replace each dot below with either 2, 3, 4, 6, or 9 to make the problem add up correctly. Each number may be used only once.

$$
\begin{array}{r}
7\,.\,.\,0 \\
+\ .\,5\,2\,6 \\
\hline
1\,.\,4\,5\,. \\
\end{array}
$$

Use a continuous series of lines to join digits whose sum equals 110. Start at "a" and finish at "b."

a

1	2	3	5	5	6	7
5	6	4	1	3	5	7
3	2	5	4	9	4	2
5	4	9	6	2	8	5
2	3	1	8	3	4	5
5	2	8	2	3	4	9
4	6	3	8	1	4	5
7	1	2	1	4	2	5
4	3	5	8	1	5	2
8	6	1	4	1	2	4
2	8	4	6	2	5	7
2	4	8	5	1	1	2
4	6	5	2	3	8	4
2	5	5	2	2	4	1

b

Naming

Five friends—Edward, Francis, George, Harry, and Isaac—built their houses around a small beach on the Atlantic Ocean. They agreed that each of them would name his house for one of the others' daughters, whose names are Elisa, Florence, Gabby, Helen, and Isabella.

To avoid giving the same name to two different houses, they decided to meet and choose together:

> George and Francis, who both wanted to call their house Helen, drew lots. Francis won. George named his house Elisa.
>
> Edward settled on Florence.
>
> Isabella's father was absent, but Isaac phoned him to tell him to name his house Gabby.
>
> Florence's father called his house Isabella.

For each man, identify his daughter's name and the name of his house.

Fill in the blanks. Each line is a logical sequence. The arrows indicate a common number.

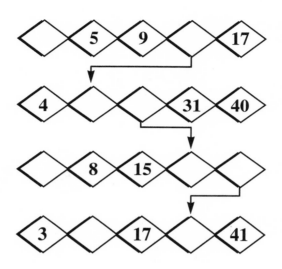

Make seven longer words from *cat* by adding letters to it. For example, by adding letters to *hat*, you can get **t**hat, hat**e**, **c**hat**ty**, **s**hat**ter**, hat**less**, hat**ch**, etc.

These words and what they represent have many properties in common but do not share all the same traits. Find seven different reasons for determining what makes one or more of these words distinct from the rest.

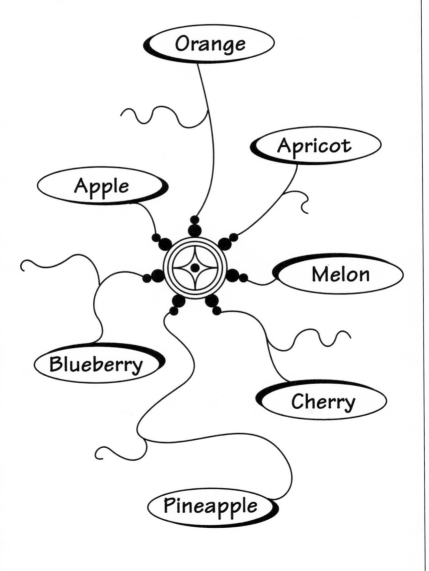

Make a word from the letters below, using each letter at least once. One letter must connect to another by a line in the diagram.

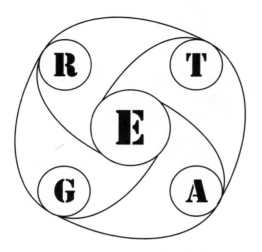

These numbers have many properties in common but do not share all the same traits. Find seven different reasons for determining what makes one or more of these numbers distinct from the rest.

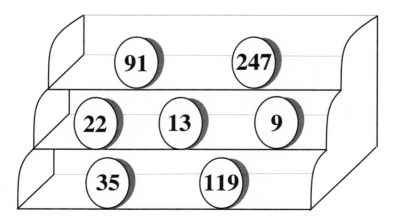

What is the missing number?

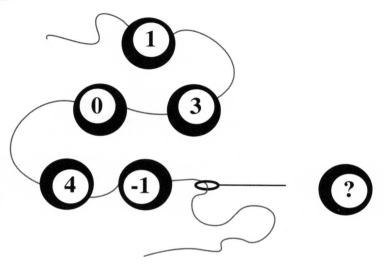

 Can you find seven shorter words that compose the long one below? For example, *intergenerational* is made up of *in, gene, ratio, era, ration*, etc.

...diplomatically...

What is the numerical relationship of the dominoes below? Which domino is missing? (Their physical arrangement is not important.)

Find seven different ways to resolve this problem.

Two ropes are hanging against a wall (at waist level). You want to hold both of them in your hands at the same time, but there is a lot of distance between them, and your arms are too short. What do you do?

Fill in the blanks. Each side of the square is a logical sequence. The arrows indicate a common number.

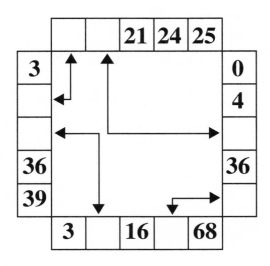

If this text were arranged alphabetically, what would the 13th word be?

With the single exception of Homer, there is no eminent writer, not even Sir Walter Scott, whom I can despise so entirely as I despise Shakespeare when I measure my mind against his. It would positively be a relief to me to dig him up and throw stones at him.

George Bernard Shaw

How many times can you read 17373? The sequence is valid only if the numbers are joined by a line.

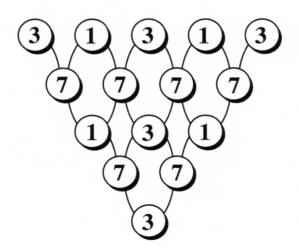

Most of the letters in this square are part of a logical pattern. However, one or more letters deviate from this pattern. Find the mistake.

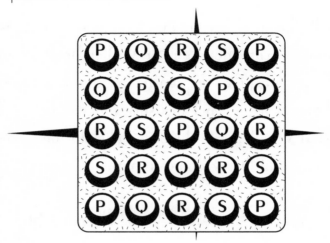

If the hexagons were placed one on top of another, what picture would you be able to see?

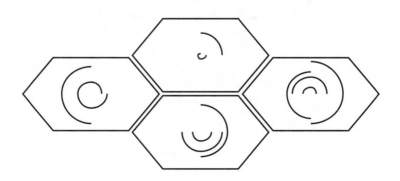

The figure on the left has ten birds spelled forward or backward, in horizontally and/or vertically connected squares, but the figure on the right has only nine of these same birds. Find all the birds and identify the one missing on the right.

E	A	G	L	E	R	A	V	E	N		C	R	A	V
C	G	K	F	L	A	M	I	N	G		R	A	N	E
R	O	R	S	F	I	N	C	H	O		O	G	E	N
A	O	O	P	O	W	L					O	S	E	E
N	S	T	A				E	R	O	T	S	H	L	
E	E	S	R		O	W	L	F	L	A	M	I	E	G
H	W	O	R		F	I	N	C	H	O	G	N	R	A
E	R	O	N		S	P	A	R	R	O	W	N	O	E

Make seven different sentences using only the words in this quote from Nigel Dennis.

This man, she reasons,
as she looks at her husband,
is a poor fish.
But he is the nearest I can get
to the big one that got away.

Follow the arrows as you fill in the blanks. Sum totals at arrows' ends must add up.

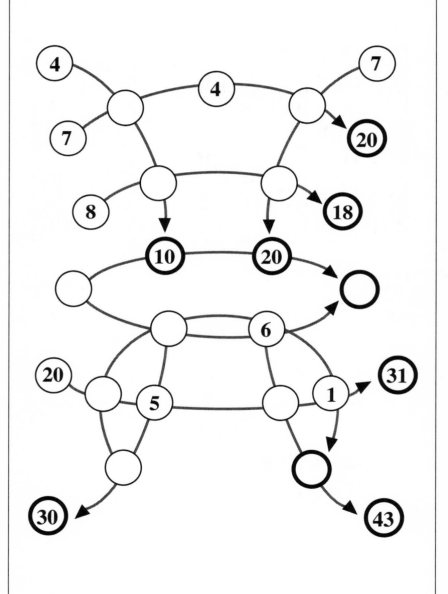

If the rectangles were placed one on top of another, what word would you be able to read?

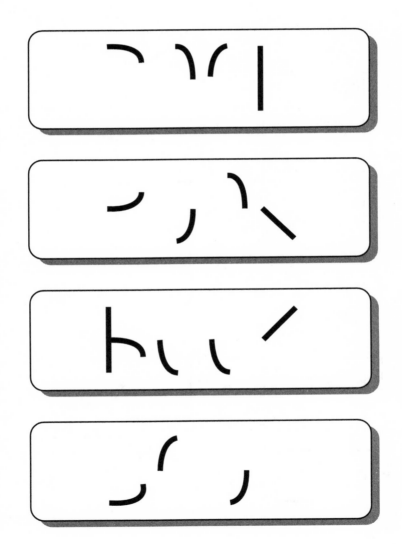

If all the diagonals were removed, how many squares and rectangles would there be in this figure?

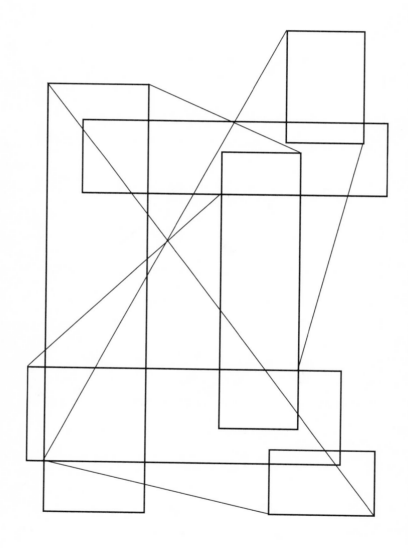

Find nine multiples of 13 on this grid. Each number is composed of a series of digits joined by line segments (or just one digit). Each digit may be used only once.

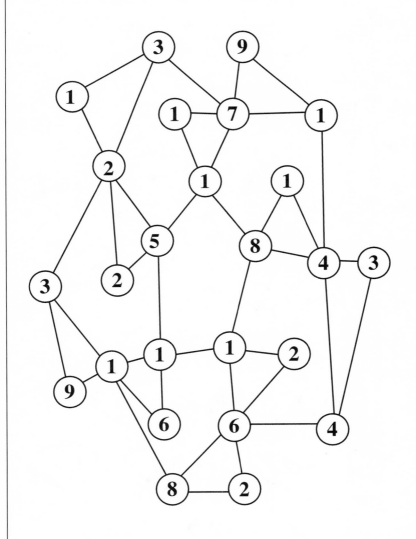

Fill in the blanks. The arrows indicate a common letter.

Yield ....

...up, down, in or out ....

Rat or rabbit ....

For Halloween ....

Connect these ten numbers. Each number may be used only once and must have no divisor in common with the following one. Connecting lines may cross over each other.

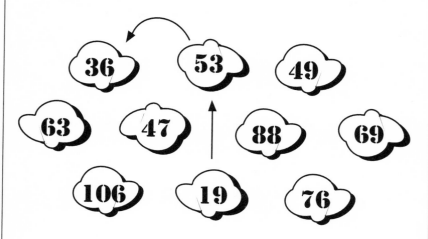

The arrows show the first two crabs in a sequence that is determined by some physical attribute(s) of the crabs. Provide the reasoning that allows the rest of the crabs to be joined in this sequence. Then give the full sequence by number. (In some cases, there may be more than one sequence that satisfies the pattern.)

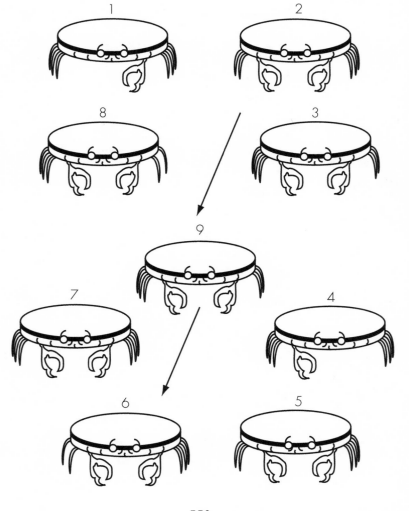

Add contiguous numbers (horizontally and vertically) so that they total 30. Each number may be used only once.

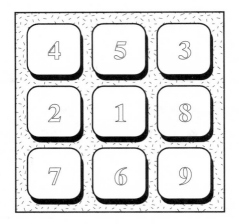

Find seven different birds beginning with at least two of these letters.

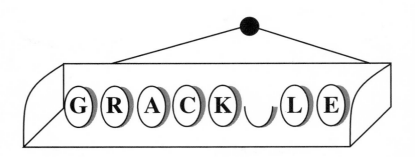

GRACKLE

What is the logical relationship or pattern of the light-face numbers below? Which boldface number fits into this relationship (and thus should be lightface)?

1	**2**	**3**	**4**	**5**	**6**	**7**
26	**25**	**24**	**23**	**22**	**21**	**8**
27	**39**	**40**	**41**	**42**	**43**	9
28	**44**	45	**46**	**47**	**48**	**10**
29	**48**	**50**	51	**52**	**53**	**11**
30	**54**	**55**	56	57	**58**	12
31	**59**	60	**61**	**62**	**63**	**13**
32	**64**	**65**	66	**67**	**68**	**14**
33	**69**	**70**	**71**	72	**73**	15
34	**74**	75	**76**	77	78	**16**
35	**79**	**80**	**81**	**64**	**83**	**17**
36	84	**85**	**86**	**87**	**88**	18
37	**89**	90	**91**	**92**	93	**19**
38	**94**	**95**	96	**97**	98	**20**

If the squares were triangles, the circles were squares, and the triangles were circles, how many

☐ circles would intersect a triangle?

☐ squares would be within a triangle?

☐ squares would intersect a circle?

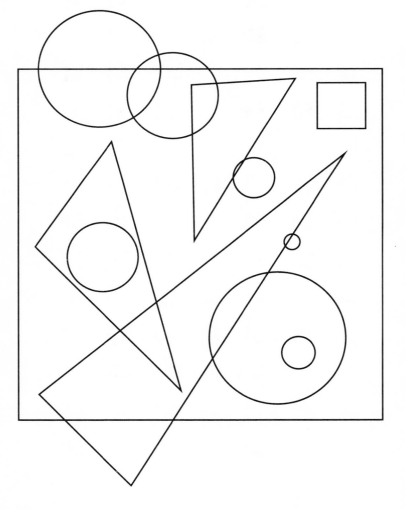

If the first square were turned upside down and placed on top of the second, you would be able to read the beginning of a sentence. After you have determined what that part of the sentence says, finish it by completing the math problem it contains.

Find the signs (+,–) that complete the equations.

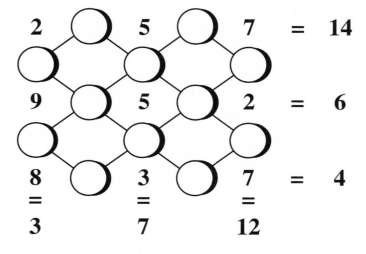

$2 \bigcirc 5 \bigcirc 7 = 14$

$9 \bigcirc 5 \bigcirc 2 = 6$

$8 \bigcirc 3 \bigcirc 7 = 4$

$8 = 3$

$3 = 7$

$7 = 12$

Using the Oscar Wilde quote directly below, decode the George Bernard Shaw quote under it. Fill in the numbered blanks with the correct letters from Wilde's like-numbered words.

IT IS ONLY SHALLOW PEOPLE WHO
1   2   3   4   5   6

DO NOT JUDGE BY APPEARANCES.
7   8   9   10   11

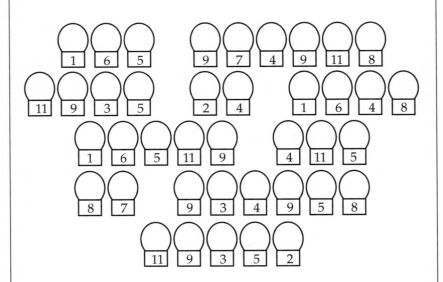

IN-LAWS

Five friends—Anthony, Ben, Christopher, David, and Eric—each have a son and a daughter. Their families are so close that each of their daughters has married one of the other four's sons.

> As a result of this bizarre situation, Anthony's son-in-law's father's daughter-in-law is Bernard's son's sister-in-law, and Christopher's daughter-in-law's father's son-in-law is David's daughter's brother-in-law.
>
> Although Bernard's daughter-in-law's father's daughter-in-law has the same mother-in-law as David's son-in-law's father's son-in-law, the situation is simplified by the fact that no daughter-in-law is her father-in-law's daughter's sister-in-law.

To whom is Eric's daughter married?

Words from a Spike Milligan quote are scattered in the frame below. Following the arrows and using each word once, fill in the blanks to reveal the quote.

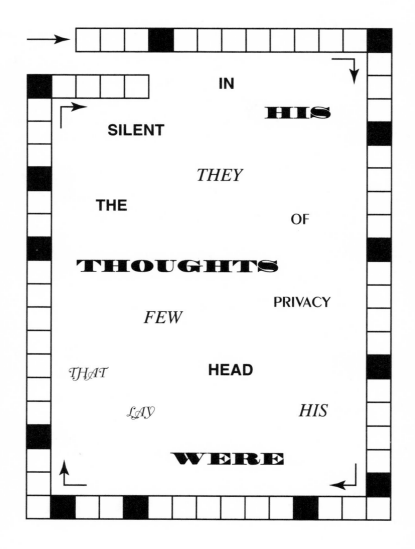

IN

HIS

SILENT

THEY

THE

OF

THOUGHTS

PRIVACY

FEW

THAT

HEAD

LAY

HIS

WERE

Connect these twelve birds. Each bird may be used only once and must have no letters in common with the following one. Connecting lines may cross over each other.

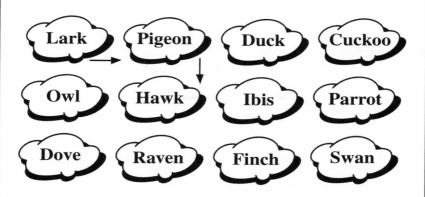

Insert +, −, x, and/or parentheses between the numbers to find the total.

1 2 3 4 5 6 7 8 9

=

33

Replace each dot below with either 2, 3, 4, 6, or 8 to make the problem add up correctly. Each number may be used only once.

$$
\begin{array}{r}
\cdot\ \cdot\ 5\ \cdot \\
+\ 9\ 4\ \cdot\ 8 \\
\hline
1\ 1\ 8\ 0\ \cdot
\end{array}
$$

Fill in the blanks above the clue in italics. Then fill in the blanks of the frame, using those same letters. The 2-headed arrows indicate a common letter.

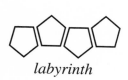

labyrinth

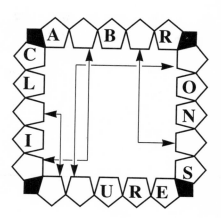

Both grids contain the same words, spelled horizontally or vertically. If a word is spelled forward in one grid, it is spelled backward in the other, except for one word, which is spelled forward in both grids. Find all the words, and identify the exceptional word.

Grid 1:

O	W	I	T	C	H
H	D	L	E	I	W
W	H	C	I	H	W
S	T	I	T	C	H
C	C	O	N	C	H
H	T	T	O	U	C	H
O	R	E	H	T	I	W	J
W	W	W	W	E	I	G	H	T
D	E	U	E	S	C	H	E	W
E	H	N	G	F
R	C	C	N	E
L	C	O	I	T
U	H	W	M	C
F	I	L	R	H	Y
H	L	E	A	I	H	G
C	D	D	H	N	W	E	W
T	I	X	C	G	C	R	Y
A	S	C	H	I	M	E	F
W	H	C	L	O	T	H	E

Grid 2:

C	C	W	E	H	C	S	E
H	H	T	H	G	I	E	W
E	I	Y	R	C	E	W	E
W	M	E	H	T	O	L	C
E	W	I	T	H	E	R
H	C	T	I	T	S
H	C	T	I	W
H	C	N	O	C
H	C	U	O	T
W	H	I	C	H
F	W	W	C	G	D	H	W	Z
V	H	H	H	N	E	S	A	C
O	Y	A	I	L	I	T	R
B	R	H	W	D	C	E
M	C	O	L	H	D
I	T	C	I	F	W
N	E	N	H	U	O
G	F	U	C	L	H
W	I	E	L	D	C

Fill in the blanks to find a Hugh Kingstill quotation. The letters of the quotation are in alphabetical order in each column of the lower figure. Going from left to right, pick a letter from each column in the lower figure to compose the quote. Skip a column when figuring a space between words, and use each letter from each column once. Some lines of the quote break in the middle of words.

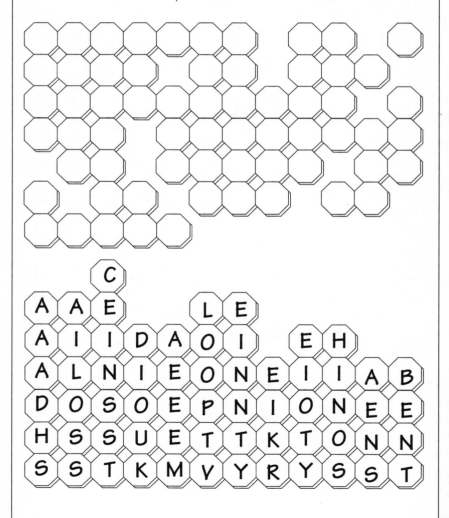

The arrows show the first two crabs in a sequence that is determined by some physical attribute(s) of the crabs. Provide the reasoning that allows the rest of the crabs to be joined in this sequence. Then give the full sequence by number. (In some cases, there may be more than one sequence that satisfies the pattern.)

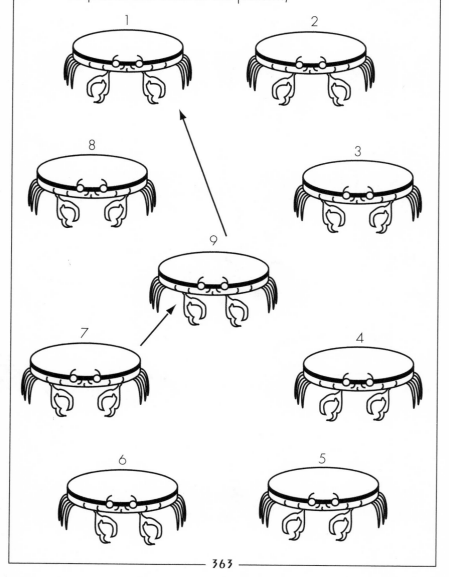

These words and what they represent have many properties in common but do not share all the same traits. Find seven different reasons for determining what makes one or more of these words distinct from the rest.

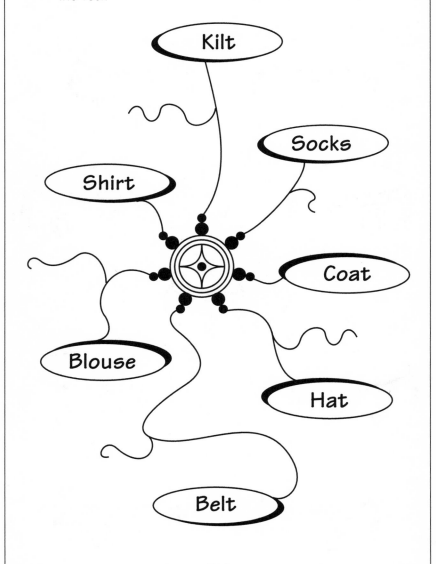

Kilt

Socks

Shirt

Coat

Blouse

Hat

Belt

If all the diagonals were removed, how many squares and rectangles would there be in this figure?

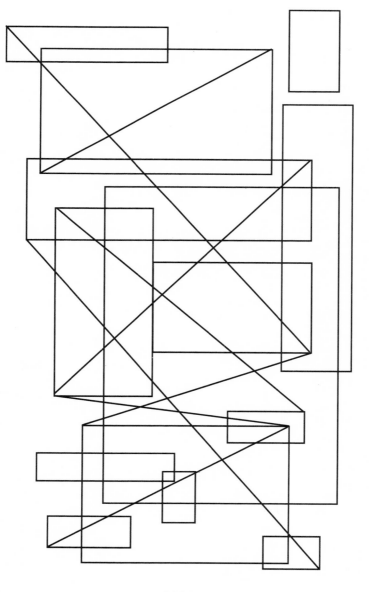

SOLUTIONS

Solutions

Page 1
31 squares and rectangles.

Page 2
The 15 on the tenth line, fifth column. All the lightface numbers are divisible by 3.

Page 3
1st: E.g., rasp, spade, hammer, rake, saw, shovel, shears.
2nd: E.g., 2 + 4 + 5 + 3 + 1 + 7 + 6 + 9 + 8 = 45.

Page 4
1st: 96.
2nd: French (an, and, and, because, bouillabaisse, by, cared, cigar, cooked, could, empty, excellent).

Page 5
1st: 2 (+ 6) 8 (+ 6) 14 (+ 6) 20 (+ 6) 26
36 (– 4) 32 (– 2) 30 (– 4) 26 (– 2) 24
32 (– 10) 22 (+ 12) 34 (– 10) 24 (+ 12) 36
8 (+ 2) 10 (+ 3) 13 (+ 4) 17 (+ 5) 22.
2nd: 7, 67: both are prime numbers
49, 7: 49 is a multiple of 7
119, 7: 119 is a multiple of 7
58, 74: both are even numbers
119, 49: both end with a 9
119, 74: the sum of their digits is the same
58, 67: the sum of their digits is the same.

Page 6
3, 9, 12, 15, 18, 21, 24, 30, 36, 39, 48.

Page 7
"No, I'm no enemy to learning; it hurts not me."

Solutions

Page 8

1st: E.g., in, dust, trial, at, ion, us, industrial.

2nd: 36 (+ 3, + 5, + 7, + 9, + 11).

Page 9

Two circles would intersect a triangle, zero squares would be within a circle, one triangle would enclose a square.

Page 10

1st: door, roams, folder, dappled.

2nd: E.g., 18, 35, 111, 28, 85, 22, 49, 51, 32, 19.

Page 11

1st: 13 (the numerical value of each first letter: M = 13, P = 16, S = 19, T = 20).

2nd: plate, mug: both are types of tableware

mug, ale: both are 3-letter words

mug, ale: ale can be drunk from a mug

glum, pale: both are expressions of emotion

glum, pale: both are 4-letter words

pale, ale: they rhyme

mug, glum: the letters of the first are all in the second.

Page 12

"Unless one is a genius, it is best to aim at being intelligible."

Page 13

1st:

1	14	22	10	18
7	20	3	11	24
13	21	9	17	5
19	2	15	23	6
25	8	16	4	12

2nd: spumanti (the only bubbly one).

Page 14

1 + 2 + 3 + 4 + 5 + 9 + 1 + 8 + 3 + 2 + 5 + 1 + 4
+ 8 + 5 + 5 + 2 + 2 + 4 + 1 = 75

Page 15

The eldest child.

Page 16

1st: 7 − 11 + 8 = 4; 4 + 8 − 3 = 9; 9 − 3 + 5 = 11;
7 + 4 − 9 = 2; 11 − 8 + 3 = 6; 8 + 3 − 5 = 6.

2nd: The sum of the six first numbers times twelve is . . . 252.

Page 17

"I do not want people to be agreeable as it saves me the trouble of liking them a great deal."

Page 18

62 squares and rectangles.

Page 19

1st: 5612 + 8743 = 14355.

2nd: *veal*: level, vowel, valid, clear.

Page 20

1st: E.g., candy, candle, scan, pelican, scandal, cane, canter.

2nd: 2 (x 2) 4 (x 2) 8 (x 2) 16 (x 2) 32
10 (+ 11) 21 (+ 11) 32 (+ 11) 43 (+ 11) 54
70 (− 9) 61 (− 9) 52 (− 9) 43 (− 9) 34
65 (− 13) 52 (− 13) 39 (− 13) 26 (− 13) 13.

Page 21

1st: 1 + 2 + 3 + 4 + 5 + 6 + 7 + 8 + 9 = 45.

2nd: E.g., purple, tan, yellow, pink, rust, olive, cyan, white, gray, blue, indigo, black.

Page 22

The dominoes progress by 2s (0, 2, 4, 6, 8, 10, 12).
The missing domino has a value of 12 (dot pattern 6:6).

Page 23

Vert.: machete, barracks, arbalest, arsenal, javelin,
assembly, crossbow, brigade, reveille, bazooka, powder,
flank, bond, stockade; horiz.: batallion, axe, eagle,
base.

Page 24

1st: E.g.: 11 is the only prime number, the only odd number,
the only number with two identical digits; 36 is the only
square; 20 is the only multiple of 5, the only multiple of
10; 42 is the only multiple of 7.

2nd: Popcorn.

Page 25

The 67 on the tenth line, fourth column, should be a
lightface number. Every third number is lightface,
following a spiral : first row left to right, last column top to
bottom, last row right to left, first column bottom to top,
second line left to right, etc.

Page 26

```
        1    2
     3  5  4  3 15
     7  6     1 14
       12     6
     9           27
        5   13
  8  1 11     1  7 28
        3   29
       19   43
```

Page 27

E.g.: Sunday is the only one named after a star, the only one composed of two words; Friday is the only one named after a goddess (Freya); Saturday is the only one named after a Roman god (Saturn), the only one named after both a god and a planet; Tuesday is the only 7-letter word; Monday is the only one named after a satellite (the Moon).

Page 28

1st: E.g., 4 + 2 + 7 + 1 + 3 + 8 = 25.

2nd: E.g., apple, pomegranate, orange, pineapple, tangerine, cranberry, raspberry.

Page 29

1st: he (and, and, be, be, belong, by, charming, differs, fact, feared, from, great).

2nd: 8.

Page 30

One circle would intersect a triangle, zero squares would be within a circle, zero triangles would enclose a square.

Page 31

1st: $(6 + 5 - 3) \times 1 \div 2 = 4$.

2nd: proficient, dexterous, adroit, competent, accomplished, practiced, adept, handy, expert.

Page 32

1st: I love women.
The constancy of the women I love is infernal.
The women I love love me.
Women who love love fickleness.
Fickleness is me!
I love the infernal fickleness of women.
Women only love constancy.

2nd: zloty, dirham, franc, penny, florin, krona, ducat, pound, mark. Dollar is missing.

Page 33

1st:

2nd: The O and the P should be reversed (the pattern is alphabetical order in a clockwise spiral).

Page 34

The number of lines on the crabs' shells are the prime numbers from 2 to 23 in order. The sequence should be 4, 9, 6, 7, 8, 2, 1, 3, 5.

Page 35

1st: $1 + (2 \times 3) + 4 + 5 + 6 + 7 + 8 + 9 = 46$.

2nd: E.g., glove, shirt, cap, blouse, cravat, shoes, kilt, gown, scarf, tie, socks, belt.

Page 36

"He was like a cock who thought the sun had risen to hear him crow."

Page 37

7, 14, 21, 28, 35, 42, 49, 56, 63, 70, 84.

Page 38

"Life is one long process of getting tired."

Page 39

22 squares and rectangles.

Page 40

LAUGH.

Solutions

Page 41

"Happy the people whose annals are blank in history books."

Page 42

1st: You show him a bus stop. You smile at him. You show him a map. You go with him. You stop a cab. You show him a policeman. You ask a passerby.

2nd: 2 (− 1) 1 (+ 3) 4 (− 2) 2 (+ 4) 6
2 (x 4) 8 (− 4) 4 (x 4) 16 (− 4) 12
12 (x 2) 24 (− 4) 20 (x 2) 40 (− 4) 36
20 (÷ 5) 4 (x 10) 40 (÷ 5) 8 (x 10) 80.

Page 43

1st: 16 (+ 1, + 2, + 3, + 4, + 5).
2nd: E.g., pen, net, rat, rating, tingly, in, tin.

Page 44

All the lightface numbers are perfect squares. The 49 on the fifth line, second column.

Page 45

1st: E.g., 127, 401, 405, 421, 211, 406, 33, 49, 29, 404.
2nd: week, elbow, belfry, reality.

Page 46

1st: water, milk: both liquids
cat, dog: both animals
doggerel, limerick: both forms of verse
melon, lime: both fruits
limerick, lime: lime begins limerick

dog, doggerel: dog begins doggerel

cat, milk: cats like milk.

2nd: 26 (the numerical value of each first letter + the number of letters: (S =19) + 5 = 24, (L = 12) + 9 = 21, (R = 18) + 9 = 27, (V = 22) + 4 = 26).

Page 47

1st: The sum of the first three odd numbers is . . . 9.

2nd: 11 + 8 − 13 = 6; 7 + 7 − 11 = 3; 6 − 9 + 4 = 1; 11 − 7 + 6 = 10; 8 − 7 + 9 = 10; 13 − 11 + 4 = 6.

Page 48

53 squares and rectangles.

Page 49

```
        10    2
     4  2  5  8  19
     9  1     3  13
        13    13
     4           30
        10    16
  14 3  4     4  3 28
        8     40
        22    60
```

Page 50

1st: riotous, tempestuous, unruly, obstreperous, boisterous, tumultuous, rowdy, refractory.

2nd: $(8 + 7 − 3) \times 2 \div 4 = 6$.

Page 51

1 + 8 + 5 + 1 + 5 + 6 + 5 + 4 + 6 + 9 + 4 + 12 + 2 + 3 + 1 + 4 + 2 + 2 = 80

Solutions

Page 52

1st: Tarok, the only game incorporating a different deck.

2nd:

30	24	18	12	6
13	7	26	25	19
21	20	14	8	27
9	28	22	16	15
17	11	10	29	23

Page 53

One circle would intersect a triangle, two triangles would be within a circle, one triangle would enclose a square.

Page 54

Beatrice has three children, Anne, two, and Caroline, one.

Page 55

1st: 1 (+ 3) 4 (+ 5) 9 (+ 7) 16 (+ 9) 25
9 (+ 8) 17 (+ 8) 25 (+ 8) 33 (+ 8) 41
41 (– 7) 34 (– 7) 27 (– 7) 20 (– 7) 13
50 (– 9) 41 (– 8) 33 (– 7) 26 (– 6) 20.

2nd: E.g., action, scion, lionize, companion, ionic, option, caption.

Page 56

Vert.: possum, puma, raccoon, whale, badger, fawn, cow, coyote, lion, calf, milk, boar, ameba;
horiz.: monkey, bobcat, cougar, rabbit, mule, pig, dragon, sponge, kitten, tiger, ameba. Ameba.

Page 57

"Nothing doth hurt more in a state than that cunning men pass for wise."

Page 58
1st: *rain*: birch, anvil, crane, cream.
2nd: 1562 + 4837 = 6399.

Page 59
1st: Gentle.
2nd: E.g.: 29 is the only prime number, the smallest number; 33 is the only number composed of two odd digits; 88 is the only multiple of 8, the only number composed of two even digits; 81 is the only multiple of 9, the only square.

Page 60
1st: 20.
2nd: heat (a, a, a, actually, and, banana, commit, conference, cuts, every, fellow, gets).

Page 61
The domino values progress by 2s (1, 3, 5, 7, 9, 11). The missing domino has a value of 11 (dot pattern 6:5).

Page 62
1st: E.g., hibiscus, may, violet, pansy, bluebell, poppy, aster, lily, rose, dahlia, peony, lilac.
2nd: 1 + 2 + 3 + 4 + 5 + 6 + 7 − 8 + 9 = 29.

Page 63
1st: E.g., pantomime, prestidigitator, singer, trapezist, pianist, trombonist, trumpetist.
2nd: E.g., 5 + 4 + 2 + 7 + 1 + 9 + 6 = 34.

Page 64
17, 37, 47, 67, 97, 127, 137, 167, 197, 367.

Page 65
1st: Adams, Polk, Truman, Monroe, Taft, Hayes, Grant, Arthur, Reagan. Ford is missing.

2nd: Enemies cannot be a choice.
Enemies cannot be too careful.
Be careful!
His choice cannot be too careful.
Be careful of his enemies too!
Be enemies of the man!
Be a man!

Page 66

The 62 on the fifth line, sixth column. All numbers surrounded by 1-digit numbers are lightface.

Page 67

32 squares and rectangles.

Page 68

E.g., February is the only one with only 28 days; October is the only whose root is numerical (*oct* means 8); June is the only one with 30 days, the only one with a solstice in it; May is the only one that also means something else ("Mother *may* I"); March is the only one with an equinox in it; January is the only one with 31 days preceded by another month with 31 days.

Page 69

"A well-written life is almost as rare as a well-spent one."

Page 70

"Cured yesterday of my disease, I died last night of my physician."

Page 71

Each of the crabs' eyes are missing alternatively, first the right eye, then the left, then the right... One valid sequence is 9, 1, 2, 3, 8, 4, 7, 5, 6.

Page 72

1st: The last line should be in reverse order: MNOP
(the pattern is alphabetical order from left to right and line
by line from top to bottom).

2nd:

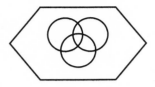

Page 73

ZENITH.

Page 74

```
        8   3
    3 4 5 6 18
    3 4   3 10
      16  12
    2       30
      15  13
  8 9 7   1 5 30
      8  50
     30  64
```

Page 75

1st: 1 (+ 2) 3 (+ 3) 6 (+ 4) 10 (+ 5) 15
2 (+ 4) 6 (+ 4) 10 (+ 4) 14 (+ 4) 18
8 (+ 6) 14 (+ 6) 20 (+ 6) 26 (+ 6) 32
10 (+ 11) 21 (+ 11) 32 (+ 11) 43 (+ 11) 54.

2nd: She can go to a shoe repair shop. She can buy a new
pair of shoes. She can break the other heel. She can sit
down and cry. She can get a strong person to carry her
home. She can take off her shoes. She can buy some
glue to try and fix it herself.

Solutions

Page 76
1st: E.g., there, the, here, her, about, bout, out.
2nd: 11 (the first prime numbers).

Page 77
1st: it (a, alone, and, cheaper, down, drag, father, full-time, how, I, I, It).
2nd: 74.

Page 78
One circle would intersect a triangle, one square would be within a circle, zero triangles would enclose a square.

Page 79
1st: melon, cantaloupe: both are varieties of squash
lemon, lime: both are citrus fruits
lemon, lime: both start with the same letter
lemon, melon: both have exactly the same letters
lemon, melon: both are 5-letter words
clementine, cantaloupe: both are 10-letter words
clementine, lime: the letters of the second are all in the first.
2nd: 19 (the numerical value of the first letter: S =19; the second letter: R = 18; the third letter: S = 19; the fourth letter: S = 19).

Page 80
1st: $13 - 24 + 12 = 1$; $11 + 7 - 8 = 10$; $9 + 13 - 14 = 8$;
$13 + 11 - 9 = 15$; $24 - 7 - 13 = 4$; $12 + 8 - 14 = 6$.
2nd: One hundred and seventy five divided by five is . . . 35.

Solutions

Page 81

Vert.: abbey, absent, excite, oar, destroy, it, book; horiz.: abrupt, adept, car, clip, tell, donkey, suffer, agonize, scream, big, aid, dew, tired, carrot, asleep, here, baby, and marry. Marry.

Page 82

"A classic is something that everybody wants to have read and nobody wants to read."

Page 83

57, 95, 114, 133, 171, 190, 209, 228.

Page 84

1st: E.g., 13, 40, 63, 22, 27, 55, 48, 49, 12, 5.
2nd: boat, arrow, famous, remains.

Page 85

1st: E.g., butcher, reporter, blacksmith, electrician, mechanic, butler, broker.
2nd: E.g., $2 + 7 + 6 + 9 + 1 + 3 + 8 = 36$.

Page 86

26 squares and rectangles.

Page 87

1st: $7 + [(8 - 5) \times 2 \div 3] = 9$.
2nd: joyful, fortunate, favorable, auspicious, blissful, blithe, cheerful, delighted, merry, ecstatic, timely.

Page 88

$7 + 8 + 7 + 6 + 5 + 4 + 3 + 2 + 1 + 2 + 3 + 4 + 5 + 6 + 7 + 1 + 1 + 1 + 1 + 1 = 75$

Page 89

For each number that appears in lightface, the reverse of it also appears in lightface. The 61 on the seventh line, third column.

Solutions

Page 90

1st: E.g., boiler, doily, spoil, foil, toil, coil, embroil.

2nd: 91 (– 18) 73 (– 18) 55 (– 18) 37 (– 18) 19

6, 19, 37, 55, 73 (6, 6 x 3 + 1, 6 x 6 + 1, 6 x 9 + 1, 6 x 12 + 1)

10 (x 2 – 1) 19 (x 2 – 1) 37 (x 2 – 1) 73 (x 2 – 1) 145

73 (+ 17) 90 (+ 19) 109 (+ 21) 130 (+ 23) 153.

Page 91

1st:

16	14	11	24	12
17	10	21	4	27
7	22	25	13	3
9	5	15	18	26
23	20	8	19	6

2nd: diving (the only watersport).

Page 92

1st: Contort.

2nd: E.g., 47 is the only prime number; 132 the only multiple of 12; 121 the only square; 105 the only multiple of 15; 910 the only multiple of 10; 152 the only multiple of 19.

Page 93

"Be wiser than other people if you can, but do not tell them so."

Page 94

The domino values progress by 1s (1, 2, 3, 4, 5, 6, 7, 8). The missing domino has a value of 6 (dot pattern 3:3, 4:2, or 5:1).

Page 95

Never.

Page 96

1st: A complaint is hard to say.
All have come to die.
Strange people had come to live.
How come strange people have it all?
Who is it?
All have to die who had to live.
People die from it.

2nd: Tennis, boxing, golf, polo, archery, kendo, judo, sumo, rugby. Diving is missing.

Page 97

1st: *care*: cheer, blaze, faces, crisp.
2nd: 5261 + 7438 = 12699.

Page 98

"I can resist everything except temptation."

Page 99

1st: $1 - 2 + 3 + 4 + (5 \times 6) + 7 + 8 + 9 = 60$.
2nd: E.g., cat, lion, bear, wolf, badger, fox, zebu, koala, deer, panda, coyote, goat.

Page 100

1st: 63.
2nd: convenient (a, a, a, abandoned, altogether, and, as, at, body, carving, casually, completion).

Page 101

```
        2     8
    7   5   4   4  20
    4  11       9  24
       18      21
    1              40
       20      19
 1  2   2       4   4  13
        8      53
       30      76
```

Page 102

1, 3, 11, 19, 59, 79, 109, 139, 149, 179, 409.

Page 103

Two circles would intersect a triangle, one square would be within a circle, one triangle would enclose a square.

Page 104

AVOID.

Page 105

21 squares and rectangles.

Page 106

1st: E.g., 3 + 1 + 7 + 6 + 9 + 8 = 34.
2nd: E.g., water polo, tennis, skiing, racing, sailing, skating, archery.

Page 107

"I could find it in my heart to marry thee, purely to be rid of thee."

Page 108

The 14 on the eighth line, seventh column. Every fifth number is lightface, following a spiral: first row left to right, second row right to left, third row left to right, etc.

Page 109

E.g.: Champagne is the only one made from grapes, the only sparkling one; sake is the only one made from rice, the only Japanese one; rum is the only one made from sugar cane; gin is the only one made from juniper berries; whisky is the only colored alcohol (amber).

Page 110

Vert.: actor, farmer, wander, batter, folder, ponder, waiter, skater, player, hinder, her, wing, cur, killer; horiz.: smoker, helper, winner, author, singer, joker, were, killer. Killer.

Page 111

1st:

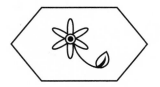

2nd: An A and a D on the fourth line should be reversed to maintain the symmetry.

Page 112

"Like a wet petal crumpled, twilight fell soddenly on the weary city."

Page 113

1st: The square root of nine plus the square of seven is . . . 52.

2nd: $11 + 4 - 9 = 6$; $3 - 8 + 7 = 2$; $4 + 8 - 7 = 5$; $11 - 3 - 4 = 4$; $4 - 8 + 8 = 4$; $9 - 7 + 7 = 9$.

Page 114

1st: 17, 23: both are prime numbers
64, 48: both are even numbers
64, 48: both are multiples of 8
64, 81: both are squares
48, 81: both are multiples of 3
51, 17: 51 is a multiple of 17
51, 81: both are multiples of 3 ending with a 1.

2nd: 36 (– 9) 27 (– 9) 18 (– 9) 9 (– 9) 0
39 (+ 6) 45 (÷ 5) 9 (+ 6) 15 (÷ 5) 3
30 (+ 3) 33 (+ 3) 36 (+ 3) 39 (+ 3) 42
21 (+ 2) 23 (+ 4) 27 (+ 6) 33 (+ 8) 41.

Page 115

1st: 14 (+ 2, + 2, + 2, + 2, + 2).

2nd: E.g., can, did, date, ate, ship, hip, candid.

Page 116

Each crab has one leg or claw less then the previous one. The sequence should be 9, 2, 8, 3, 6, 5, 4, 1, 7.

Page 117

1st: nana, organ, doctor, florist.

2nd: E.g., 8, 11, 81, 26, 123, 17, 22, 21, 74, 99.

Page 118

1st: 29 (the numerical value of the first consonant + the numerical value of each first vowel: C + I = 12, D + U = 25, R + O = 33, N + O = 29).

2nd: bay, window: they form the term *bay windows*
bay, ocean: both are bodies of water
bay, sky: both are 3-letter words ending in Y
pane, window: they form the word *window pane*
boat, ocean: boats sail on the ocean
pane, plane: they rhyme
plane, sky: planes fly in the sky.

Page 119

$$2 + 7 + 1 + 3 + 5 + 2 + 3 + 10 + 7 + 1 + 1 + 1 + 1 + 4 + 2 + 5 + 5 + 3 + 4 + 3 + 7 + 3 = 80$$

Page 120

1st: dissemble, allege, feign, simulate, profess, imagine, fake, claim, aspire, act.

2nd: $(6 + 5 - 9) \times 4 \div 8 = 1$.

Page 121

1st: objects (and, art, as, baskets, craftsmanship, gives, gives, imagination, imagination, is, many, modern).

2nd: 8.

Solutions

Page 122

```
        6   1
      6 3 6 5 20
     11 7   3 21
        16  9
      8        33
        15  10
    2 8 14  10 11 45
        7   51
       36   71
```

Page 123

11, 66, 143, 374, 286, 385.

Page 124

25 squares and rectangles.

Page 125

1st: 5, 7, 11, 13, 17 (prime numbers from 5 to 17)
10, 6, 13, 1, 13 (the numerical value of the first letter of
the first five months: j, f, m, a, m)
12 (+ 1) 13 (– 4) 9 (+ 1) 10 (– 4) 6
50 (– 40) 10 (+ 30) 40 (– 20) 20 (+ 10) 30.
2nd: E.g., feather, weather, sheath, great, heat, cheat, seat.

Page 126

One circle would intersect a triangle, zero squares would
be within a circle, zero triangles would enclose a square.

Page 127

1st: E.g., tea, gin, eggnog, tonic, tequila, coffee, lemonade.
2nd: E.g., 7 + 2 + 4 + 1 + 9 + 8 + 3 + 5 = 39.

Page 128

"A sharp tongue is the only edged tool that grows keener
with constant use."

Solutions

Page 129

1st: E.g.: 3 is the only prime number, the only number that divides 4 of the others; 96 is the only multiple of 12; 9 is the only square; 14 is the only multiple of 7; 50 is the only multiple of 10; 27 is the only cube.

2nd: Wayward.

Page 130

1st: penguin (the only one that is not a mammal).

2nd:

25	11	9	19	18
22	7	24	12	16
10	17	27	23	13
21	20	15	6	26
8	28	5	29	14

Page 131

"Money speaks sense in a language all nations understand."

Page 132

Roast beef and apple pie.

Page 133

The lightface numbers in each column add up to 80. The 8 on the third line, sixth column.

Page 134

1st: E.g., piano, lute, organ, bell, harp, violin, drum, oboe, trumpet, banjo, fife, horn.

2nd: $1 + 2 + (3 \times 4) + 5 + 6 + 7 + 8 + 9 = 50$.

Page 135

The dominoes progress so that the difference between the dots on each side of each domino is 1 (6 dots − 5 dots on the 11-dot domino), 2 (6 − 4), 3 (3 − 0), 4 (5 − 1), 5 (5 − 0), 6 (6 − 0). The missing domino has a "difference value" of 6 (dot pattern 6:0).

Page 136

1st: 2 + 4 + 8 = 14; 3 − 3 + 6 = 6; 5 + 7 − 7 = 5; 2 − 3 + 5 = 4; 4 + 3 − 7 = 0; 8 + 6 + 7 = 21.
2nd: Eight times nine divided by the sum of two and ten is . . . 6.

Page 137

"An expert is one who knows more and more about less and less."

Page 138

E.g.: Tennis is the only individual sport, the only one played with a racket; hockey is the only one played on ice, the only one played with a puck; rugby is the only one played with an oval ball, the only one played with both hands and feet; basketball is the only one with a basket.

Page 139

1st: claret, tea, juice, soda, vodka, water, beer, milk, ale, syrup, coffee. Gin is missing.
2nd: He is fond of people.
People want things.
He is fond of giving things he does not use to people.
People use them for making things.
He is not fond of them.
People want things which have no use.
Which things does he want to use?

Page 140

1st: 12.

2nd: he (a, acquired, arm, behind, behind, by, clearing, difficult, even, existence, flourish, had).

Page 141

COLD.

Page 142

13, 65, 91, 156, 169, 182, 208, 221.

Page 143

51 squares and rectangles.

Page 144

1st: The F and G should be reversed (the pattern is each line is in alphabetical order with the two middle letters reversed).

2nd:

Page 145

Vert.: hale, hair, hand, face, percolator, mail, coil, bath, lash, boil, egg, chariot; horiz.: tooth, death, grain, eagle, broom, winter, cleaner, altimeter, barometer, vein, acid, but, chariot. Chariot.

Page 146

1st: E.g., 2 + 7 + 6 + 9 + 8 + 3 = 35.

2nd: E.g., carrot, cauliflower, artichoke, radish, asparagus, romaine, celery.

Page 147

```
        6    3
     8  1  10  1  20
     4  7      9  20
        14     13
     3            30
        6     21
  17 1  9      1  6  34
        7     41
       22     63
```

Page 148

1st: E.g., not, with, stand, wit, it, standing, tan.
2nd: 2 (1, 2, 3, 4, 5, 6 in alphabetical order).

Page 149

"A plausible impossibility is always preferable to an unconvincing possibility."

Page 150

1st: lake, adept, ballet, exhibit.
2nd: E.g., 15, 32, 33, 31, 122, 123, 49, 48, 121, 27

Page 151

One circle would intersect a triangle, zero squares would be within a circle, two triangles would enclose a square.

Page 152

The 14 on the fourteenth line, second column. Each lightface number says how many numbers you need to move forward to get the next lightface number, etc.

Page 153

1st: 1 (+ 1) 2 (+ 1) 3 (+ 1) 4 (+ 1) 5
2 (+ 2) 4 (+ 2) 6 (+ 2) 8 (+ 2) 10
2 (+ 1) 3 (+ 3) 6 (+ 5) 11 (+ 7) 18
1 (+ 1) 2 (+ 2) 4 (+ 3) 7 (+ 4) 11.

2nd: 61, 16: both are composed of the same two digits
44, 11: both are composed of one repeated digit
44, 11: 44 is a multiple of 11
16, 32: 32 is a multiple of 16
32, 44: both are multiples of 4
32, 44: both are even numbers
39, 89: both have the same second digit.

Page 154

"Straightfaced in his cunning sleep, he pulls the legs of his dreams."

Page 155

1st: 9 (the numerical value of the last vowel: I = 9, I = 9, I = 9, I = 9).

2nd: bottle, water: they form the word *water bottle*
bottle, lobe: the letters of the second are all in the first
bottle, bowl: both are containers for liquids
cloud, water: clouds are water vapor
cloud, gas: gas can be seen in clouds
lobe, nose: both are facial features
joke, gas: "It's a gas!" and *joke* both relate to having fun.

Page 156

3 + 12 + 17 + 18 + 15 + 4 + 11 + 10 + 9 + 8 + 7 + 6 + 2 + 20 + 13 + 6 + 7 + 2 = 170

Solutions

Page 157

Each of the whole crabs is alternated with one of those that has something new missing. One valid sequence is 1, 3, 8, 4, 7, 9, 6, 5.

Page 158

"They spend their time mostly looking forward to the past."

Page 159

1st: $(9 + 8 - 3) \times 2 \div 4 = 7$.

2nd: immutable, continual, regular, ceaseless, perpetual, invariable, stable, dependable, incessant, loyal, steady.

Page 160

1st: E.g., shower, chowder, howl, however, anyhow, show, chow.

2nd: 2 (+ 2) 4 (+ 2) 6 (+ 2) 8 (+ 2) 10
2 (+ 2) 4 (+ 2) 6 (− 2) 4 (− 2) 2
1 (+ 1) 2 (+ 2) 4 (+ 3) 7 (+ 4) 11
6 (+ 5) 11 (− 4) 7 (+ 3) 10 (− 2) 8.

Page 161

1st: is (a, as, be, but, buys, buys, cheaper, cow, do, in, is, is).

2nd: 576.

Page 162

21 squares and rectangles.

Page 163

34, 51, 68, 85, 187, 374, 408.

Page 164

1st: E.g.: 23 is the only prime number; 56 is the only multiple of 7; 144 is the only square, the only multiple of 12; 55 is the only one composed of one repeated digit; 110 is the only multiple of 10; 216 is the only cube.

2nd: Games or Mages.

Solutions

Page 165

1st: E.g., rhinoceros, gazelle, hare, horse, goat, raccoon, whale.

2nd: E.g., $1 + 3 + 6 + 8 + 5 + 7 + 4 + 9 = 43$.

Page 166

"That vice pays hommage to virtue is notorious; we call it hypocrisy."

Page 167

1st:

21	27	8	9	15
13	14	20	26	7
25	6	12	18	19
17	23	24	5	11
4	10	16	22	28

2nd: cedar (the only evergreen).

Page 168

```
            7       7
        4   6   8   1   19
        4   5       6   15
            18      14
        3               35
            17      15
    10  3   7       6   4   30
            1       40
            25      61
```

Page 169

1st: One hundred and forty four is the square of . . . 12.

2nd: $8 + 7 - 6 = 9$; $9 + 9 + 9 = 27$; $7 - 6 + 9 = 10$; $8 + 9 - 7 = 10$; $7 + 9 - 6 = 10$; $6 + 9 - 9 = 6$.

Page 170

The dominoes progress so that for each domino whose two sides are of the same value there is another domino of the same total value (1:1 = 2:0, 3:3 = 5:1, 5:5 = 6:4). The missing domino has a value of 10 (dot pattern 6:4).

Page 171

1st: $(1 + 2) \times 3 - 4 - 5 + 6 + 7 + 8 + 9 = 30$.

2nd: E.g., pepper, mint, sage, curry, dill, nutmeg, basil, thyme, paprika, fennel, tarragon, chives.

Page 172

1st: Time puzzles me.
Time them!
Think about nothing.
I think about space, and nothing troubles me more.
I think less about space than time.
I think about nothing more than nothing.
Space puzzles me, yet nothing troubles me.

2nd: banjo, harp, violin, piano, cornet, bell, drum, trumpet, organ. Guitar is missing.

Page 173

1st: $1357 + 6439 = 7796$.

2nd: *weak*: bleak, koala, yawns, weedy.

Page 174

Vert.: feline, ermine, chain, outline, concubine, fine, wine, dime, spine, train, quinine; horiz.: ravine, vermin, dine, fin, win, saline, if, undine, line, opine, blind, grain, plain. Quinine.

Page 175

E.g.: Snake is the only one that doesn't start with the same letter as any of the others, the only reptile, the only egg-layer; possum is the only marsupial; puma is the only feline; dolphin is the only marine mammal; deer is the only one with antlers.

Page 176

SEARCH.

Page 177

All the lightface numbers are prime. The 47 on the ninth line, fourth column.

Page 178

Four circles would intersect a triangle, one square would be within a circle, zero triangles would enclose a square.

Page 179

"I like work: it fascinates me. I can sit and look at it for hours."

Page 180

1st: 140.

2nd: nothing (a, a, all, are, are, at, catalogue, entertaining, half, I, more, much).

Page 181

28 squares and rectangles.

Page 182

1, 2, 11, 17, 23, 41, 61,151, 181, 211.

Page 183

1st:

2nd: The B and the Y in the first column should be reversed. (The pattern is down the columns, from left to right, the letters fill in every other circle alphabetically; the rest of the circles are filled in alphabetically up the columns from right to left).

Page 184

1st: E.g., 3 + 5 + 4 + 2 + 7 + 6 + 1 + 8 = 36.

2nd: E.g., cart, car, ship, scooter, canoe, raft, shuttle.

Page 185

1st: 11 (+2, +2, +2, +2, +2).

2nd: E.g., war, are, house, man, use, ware, warehouse.

Page 186

1st: You buy him an alarm clock. You give a bonus for punctuality. You reduce his pay by the amount of time he arrived late. You call him every morning to wake him up. You get him to live closer to the office. You set all his clocks forward. You change his working hours.

2nd: 2, 3, 5, 7, 11 (prime numbers from 2 to 11)
5, 15, 30, 45, 60 [5 (x 3) (x 6) (x 9) (x 12)]
60 (− 12) 48 (− 12) 36 (− 12) 24 (− 12) 12
15 (÷ 5) 3 (x 4) 12 (÷ 3) 4 (x 2) 8.

Page 187

"He never does a proper thing without giving an improper reason for it."

Page 188

1st: mouth, jug: both have round openings
mouth, scream: screams are emitted by mouths
mouth, eyes: both are facial features
cry, eyes: eyes cry tears
potato, eyes: potatoes have eyes
cry, scream: both are expressions of anger or despair
cry, jug: both are 3-letter words.

2nd: 8 (+1 in alphabetical order, starting at 5 for Corn).

Page 189

1st: E.g., 112, 57, 68, 35, 99, 43, 119, 30, 53, 34.

2nd: tool, petal, damsel, mankind.

Page 190

1st: $2 + 9 - 6 = 5$; $4 - 1 + 8 = 11$; $7 - 5 + 9 = 11$;
$2 + 4 + 7 = 13$; $9 + 1 - 5 = 5$; $6 + 8 - 9 = 5$.

2nd: Nine and four minus the product of six times two is . . . 1.

Page 191

```
          8     1
      9  1 14  3 27
      8  7     7 22
         16   11
      3           30
         14   13
   10 3  9     3  5 30
         10   45
         33   61
```

Page 192

1st: error, misjudge, gaffe, blunder, oversight, misconstrue, misunderstand, misstep.

2nd: $[9 + 8 - (5 \times 1)] \div 2 = 6$.

Page 193

"Pleasure is after all a safer guide than either right or duty."

Page 194

1st: orange (the only citrus fruit).

2nd:

17	9	21	13	30
11	28	20	7	24
10	22	14	26	18
29	16	8	25	12
23	15	27	19	6

Page 195

1st: 19, 13, 7, 3, 1 (every second prime number in reverse order)

7, 11, 13, 17, 19 (the prime numbers from 7 to 19)

7, 17, 37, 47, 67 (prime numbers ending in 7)

19 (+9) 28 (+9) 37 (+9) 46 (+9) 55.

2nd: E.g., nauseate, seam, search, seal, season, seat, seamstress.

Page 196

As the numbers progress consecutively, each new lightface number increases by one more unit than the previous one (1 + 1 = 2 + 2 = 4 + 3 = 7... + 13 = 92). The 2 on the first line, second column.

Page 197

10 + 3 + 5 + 6 + 7 + 8 + 9 + 10 + 17 + 30 + 24 + 10 + 3 + 13 + 5 + 15 + 5 + 20 + 9 + 1 = 210

Page 198

4. (One man and his sister. One of them has a son and one of them has a daughter—it doesn't matter which has which.)

Page 199

1st: Cents or sentence.

2nd: E.g., 64 is the only even number, the only multiple of 8, the only square; 65 is the only multiple of 5; 21 is the only multiple of 7; 27 is the only multiple of 9; 223 is the only one greater than the sum of any two of the others.

Page 200

34 squares and rectangles.

Page 201

Vert.: later, plough, reaper, noise, mower, latin, clown; horiz.: table, motif, adore, stamp, means, shadow, peeler, blower, cutter, dredge, engine, abolish, packer, spinner. Spinner.

Page 202

"It was a book to kill time for those who like it better dead."

Page 203

Two circles would intersect a triangle, three squares would be within a circle, one triangle would enclose a square.

Page 204

1st: *jest*: stare, joint, najas, tress.

2nd: $6521 + 7976 = 14497$.

Page 205

The dominoes progress so that a domino with a blank alternates with one without and the sum of the dots on each of the dominoes is 1, 2, 3, 4, 5, 6. The missing domino has a value of 1 (dot pattern 0:1).

Page 206

1st: E.g., apple, kiwi, grape, litchi, orange, plum, cherry, banana, lime, guava, berry, mango.

2nd: $1 + 2 - 3 + 4 + 5 + 6 + (7 \times 8) + 9 = 80$.

Solutions

Page 207

1st: Beckett, Lang, Wilde, Twain, Aiken, Mann, Amis, Saki, Eliot, Hardy. Waugh is missing.

2nd: People judge by appearances.
        Do not judge.
        It is shallow.
        Who is only shallow?
        Who is it?
        Judge it not by appearances.
        Is it only shallow people who judge by appearances?

Page 208

Alternate the crab with the least remaining dots with the one with the most remaining dots. The sequence should be 1, 8, 2, 9, 6, 4, 7, 5, 3.

Page 209

1st: London (amount, bad, clean, flirt, husbands, in, in, is, is, It, It, linen).

2nd: 64.

Page 210

"Fortune is full of fresh variety: constant in nothing but inconstancy."

Page 211

1st: E.g., carmine, tan, ecru, red, crimson, lavender, sable.

2nd: E.g., 5 + 6 + 3 + 8 + 4 + 9 + 7 = 42.

Page 212

```
            10    1
        4  3  8  5  20
        4  7     6  17
           20    12
        9              41
           11    21
    14  9  7      8  4  42
           8     53
           26    82
```

Page 213

3, 17, 23, 43, 61, 83, 103, 223.

Page 214

1st: E.g., fun, fund, dam, dame, men, tall, tally.
2nd: 21 (+2, +3, +4, +5, +6).

Page 215

LIZARD.

Page 216

1st: The second A and the second B should be reversed (the pattern is each horizontal line is symmetrical).

2nd:

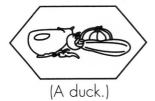

(A duck.)

Page 217

The 32 on the fifth line, fourth column. The lightface numbers are numbers following a prime number.

Page 218

1st: E.g., 21, 22, 57, 25, 42, 65, 24, 35, 51, 62.
2nd: pail, plump, mutate, blatant.

Page 219

18 squares and rectangles.

Page 220

Three circles would intersect a triangle, one square would be within a circle, one triangle would enclose a square.

Page 221

"A truth that's told with bad intent beats all the lies you can invent."

Page 222

"In silence they stood, in mortal silence, under that immortal snow-dark silent sky."

Page 223

1st: The square root of two hundred and twenty five is . . . 15.

2nd: $3 + 6 + 6 = 15$; $8 + 6 - 11 = 3$; $7 - 9 + 5 = 3$;
$3 + 8 - 7 = 4$; $6 + 6 - 9 = 3$; $6 - 11 + 5 = 0$.

Page 224

1st: E.g., $3 + 5 + 4 + 2 + 1 + 8 + 9 + 6 = 38$.

2nd: E.g., Carroll, Aiken, Blake, Bradbury, Brontë, Cervantes, Bierce.

Page 225

"She had a penetrating sort of laugh, rather like a train going into a tunnel."

Page 226

Vert.: galaxy, acceptability, penicillin, tomb, ban, game; horiz.: hurt, milk, wine, yoghurt, soul, nail, coffee, drawers, circus, ball, pub, trellis, checked. Checked.

Page 227

1st: 28 (– 7) 21 (+ 5) 26 (– 3) 23 (+ 1) 24
22 (+ 4) 26 (+ 8) 34 (+ 4) 38 (+ 8) 46
37 (+ 1) 38 (– 2) 36 (+ 3) 39 (– 4) 35
12 (+ 12) 24 (+ 12) 36 (+ 12) 48 (+ 12) 60.

2nd: You hitchhike. You give up. You call a garage. You repair with the kit you always have on you. You call a tow truck. You push your bike to the nearest town. You kick your bike a few times, then abandon it on the side of the road; it'll just have to find its own way home.

Page 228

1st: 48.

2nd: of (Ambition, and, and, and, Arithmetic, begin, branches, course, Derision, different, Distraction, Mock).

Page 229

1st: cat, scratch: cats scratch

cat, scratch: the letters of the first are all in the second

cat, cream: the cat got at the cream

cat, mint: catrip is a kind of mint

milk, cream: cream comes from milk

milk, mint: both are 4-letter words beginning with M

milk, silk: they rhyme.

2nd: 10 (the number of letters in each desert).

Page 230

$$1 + 3 + 4 + 5 + 4 + 3 + 2 + 1 + 0 + 4 + 2 + 1 + 1$$
$$+ 2 + 3 + 1 + 3 + 1 + 3 + 1 + 2 + 4 + 2 + 2 + 0 +$$
$$6 + 5 + 4 + 8 + 2 = 80$$

Page 231

	1	4		
5	7	8	6	26
4	2		14	20
	10	24		
1			35	
	19	15		
8	3	9	7	3	30
	7	47		
	35	69		

Page 232

7, 14, 21, 35, 56, 70, 91, 98, 112, 210.

Page 233

1st: $8 + 9 - (3 \times 1) \div 2 = 7$.

2nd: ludicrous, nonsensical, daft, silly, senseless, injudicious, idiotic, ridiculous, imprudent, unwise, absurd.

Page 234

1st: E.g., stingy, stink, tine, instinct, patina, matinee, tingle.

2nd: 3 (+ 10) 13 (+ 10) 23 (+ 10) 33 (+ 10) 43
 9 (+ 4) 13 (+ 5) 18 (+ 6) 24 (+ 7) 31
 2 (+ 11) 13 (– 3) 10 (+ 11) 21 (– 3) 18
 21 (– 12) 9 (+ 9) 18 (– 6) 12 (+ 3) 15.

Page 235

1st:

9	22	11	23	26
29	21	18	8	12
6	16	28	25	10
30	7	24	13	20
15	27	14	17	19

2nd: cello (the only string instrument).

Page 236

1st: Clever.

2nd: E.g., 64 is the only square, the only even number; 133 is the only multiple of 7, the only odd number not also a prime number, the only multiple of 19, the only multiple of 2 prime numbers; 71 is the only odd number the sum of whose digits is even.

Page 237

Andrew's boat is the Seagull.
Bertram's boat is the Faithful.
Charles' boat is the Mary Jane.

Solutions

Page 238

33 squares and rectangles.

Page 239

1st: *fast*: staff, flail, taffy, taste.
2nd: 2191 + 4376 = 6567.

Page 240

The lightface numbers consist of twelve numbers: six numbers that have swapped position with six other numbers and are therefore out of sequence. The 60 on the third line, first column.

Page 241

E.g., piano is the only one that can't be carried, the only keyboard instrument; violin is the only one played with a bow; drum is the only percussion instrument that is a basic member of an orchestra; flute is the only woodwind; trumpet is the only brass; guitar is the only one whose strings are both strummed and plucked.

Page 242

"The silence went straight from rapt to fraught without pausing at pregnant."

Page 243

Two circles would intersect a triangle, one triangle would be within a circle, three triangles would intersect a circle.

Page 244

The dominoes progress so that the sum of the dots on each of the dominoes, alternating doubles with dominoes with blanks, is 1, 2, 3, 4, 5, 6. The missing domino has a value of 6 or 0 (dot pattern 3:3 or 0:0).

Page 245

1st: E.g., fir, coconut, fig, cedar, rowan, orange tree, copper beech.

2nd: E.g., $1 + 7 + 4 + 9 + 2 + 8 + 6 = 37$.

Page 246

1st: Only I can shut the doors.
I shut the doors to life.
The doors of many apartments can shut.
Shut the doors!
Yet can I describe life?
Can I rest?
I can only describe life as shut doors to large apartments.

2nd: dagger, sword, saber, rapier, sling, flail, lance, spear.
Glaive is missing.

Page 247

1st: 20 (10, 20, 30, 40, 50, 60 in alphabetical order).

2nd: E.g., her, here, ere, in, aft, after, rein.

Page 248

"Bigotry may be roughly defined as the anger of men who have no opinions."

Page 249

1st:

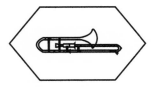

2nd: The A on the second line, second column and the C on the third line, third column should be reversed (the pattern is a symmetrical arrangement of each upper-left to lower-right diagonal).

Page 250

PLAY.

Page 251

1st: film, motif, bonsai, certain.
2nd: E.g., 24, 35, 51, 20, 33, 14, 15, 44, 21, 68.

Page 252

```
          3     9
      8  4  1  4  17
      7  7     7  21
         14    20
      9             43
         20    14
   13 12 3      6  6  40
         8    60
        31    80
```

Page 253

1st: mother (all, dripping, electricity, her, her, horrible, house, in, invisibly, latter, life, lived).
2nd: 8.

Page 254

Two squares would intersect a circle, two squares would intersect a triangle, one triangle would enclose a circle.

Page 255

14 squares and rectangles.

Page 256

1st: $11 + 7 - 8 = 10$; $10 + 7 + 8 = 25$; $13 + 9 + 9 = 31$;
 $11 - 10 + 13 = 14$; $7 - 7 + 9 = 9$; $8 + 8 + 9 = 25$.
2nd: Thirteen times the square root of sixteen is . . . 52.

Page 257

"For fools rush in where angels fear to tread."

Page 258

1st: E.g., $6 + 2 + 5 + 8 + 4 + 1 + 7 = 33$.
2nd: E.g., aster, marigold, magnolia, mimosa, japonica, snowdrop, narcissus.

Page 259

3, 9, 12, 21, 33, 48, 84, 126, 162, 192.

Page 260

1st: 16 (the numerical value of the first consonant: T = 20, V = 22, S = 19, P = 16).
2nd: acute, hairy: both are 5-letter words
acute, dumb: they are antonyms
acute, mute: they rhyme
dumb, mute: they are synonyms
dumb, mute: both are 4-letter words
head, hairy: they start with the same consonant
air, hairy: the first word is in the second.

Page 261

Vert.: evasion, pan, dynamic, cunning, hairy, ill, wise, strong, dainty, languid, out; horiz.: charm, beauty, kind, weak, fat, dab, happy, shyness, lonely, afraid, guilt, emotion, zesty, out. Out.

Page 262

1st: 61, 73: both are prime numbers
22, 11: both are composed of one repeated digit
11, 22: 22 is a multiple of 11
42, 63: both are multiples of 7
54, 63: both are multiples of 9
54, 63: the sum of their digits equals 9
42, 54: both are multiples of 6.

2nd: 21 (+ 11) 32 (+ 12) 44 (+ 13) 57 (+ 14) 71
36 (+ 8) 44 (+ 12) 56 (+ 16) 72 (+ 20) 92
87 (– 15) 72 (– 11) 61 (– 15) 46 (– 11) 35
59 (– 13) 46 (+ 12) 58 (– 11) 47 (+ 10) 57.

Page 263

"Life was a funny thing that happened to me on the way to the grave."

Page 264

1st: pertinent, rational, wise, cogent, valid, reasonable, judicious, sound, coherent, relevant, obvious.
2nd: $(6 + 5 - 9) \times 4 \div 1 = 8$.

Page 265

All the lightface numbers are prime. The 23 on the fourteenth line, fifth column.

Page 266

1st: emu (the only flightless bird).

2nd:

14	12	9	22	10
15	8	19	2	25
5	20	23	11	1
7	3	13	16	24
21	18	6	17	4

Page 267

"This is not a novel to be tossed aside lightly; it should be thrown with great force."

Page 268

Yes.

Page 269

1 + 3 + 4 + 9 + 17 + 16 + 10 + 9 + 11 + 20 + 1 +
4 + 5 + 10 + 20 + 15 + 5 + 8 + 2 + 3 + 1 + 1 + 25
+ 31 + 9 + 4 + 4 + 4 + 8 + 3 + 6 + 1 = 270

Page 270

1st: 16.

2nd: heard (a, a, a, a, and, as, brick, carried, encourage, had, have, he).

Page 271

1st: 1 (+ 2) 3 (− 3) 0 (+ 2) 2 (− 3) −1
0 (+ 4) 4 (− 2) 2 (+ 4) 6 (− 2) 4
0 (+ 4) 4 (+ 2) 6 (+ 4) 10 (+ 2) 12
11 (+ 8) 19 (− 7) 12 (+ 6) 18 (− 5) 13.

2nd: E.g., where, were, heretic, severe, centered, mere, perennial.

Page 272

1st: 9756 + 1358 = 11114.

2nd: *quit*: quilt, moist, quote, equal.

Page 273

1st: E.g., 85 is the only multiple of 5, the only mutiple of 17; 256 is the only even number, the only square; 231 is the only multiple of 11, the only multiple of 3, the only multiple of 7.

2nd: Coconut.

Page 274

27 squares and rectangles.

Page 275

```
      5    3
           4
  8 9 7  1 25
  6 8    6 20
    22   10
  1          33
    15   17
4 9 13    3  1 30
     8   50
    36   70
```

Page 276

1, 4, 9, 16, 36, 64, 121, 144, 225, 676, 784.

Page 277

Two circles would intersect a triangle, five triangles would be within a square, three triangles would intersect a square.

Page 278

"I would have answered your letter sooner, but you didn't send one."

Page 279

The dominoes progress so that the product of the dots on each side of each domino is 0 (0^2), 1 (1^2), 4 (2^2), 9 (3^2), 16 (4^2), 25 (5^2). The missing domino has a value of 16 (dot pattern 4:4).

Page 280

E.g.: One is the only one that is also its own square, the only one that equally divides all the others, the only one that begins with O; two is the only one that is even and prime, the only one whose square is one of the others; six is the only one that is a product of three of the others; seven is the only odd number that doesn't end in e.

Page 281
1st: E.g., harmonica, bassoon, horn, bugle, banjo, harp, bagpipes.

2nd: E.g., $6 + 3 + 4 + 7 + 5 + 2 = 27$.

Page 282
1st: E.g., kin, kind, hear, ear, art, heart, he.

2nd: 19 (the prime numbers from 5 to 19).

Page 283
1st: Brazil, Japan, Ghana, Gabon, Egypt, Italy, Mexico, France, Russia. Peru is missing.

2nd: That thief has the treasure.

First stop the thief.

He that cries first is out.

He cries out that he has the treasure.

Stop thief!

"The treasure is stolen!" he cries.

He is the first that cries.

Page 284
1st: The second B and the second C on the last line should be reversed (the pattern is on each line the first two letters are the same as the last two letters).

2nd:

Page 285
GAMES.

Page 286
The 62 on the fifth line, sixth column. Every lightface number is surrounded by one-digit numbers.

Page 287

1st: The sum of the first seven even numbers including 0 is . . . 42.

2nd: 3 + 4 − 5 = 2; 7 − 3 + 5 = 9; 3 − 1 + 9 = 11;
3 + 7 − 3 = 7; 4 + 3 − 1 = 6; 5 + 5 − 9 = 1.

Page 288

1st: calm, alack, weaken, knotted.

2nd: E.g., 61, 487, 499, 48, 613, 96, 35, 81, 37, 27.

Page 289

"Oozing charm from every pore, he oiled his way around the floor."

Page 290

"A noisy man is always in the right."

Page 291

1st: met (another, asked, but, but, but, but, but, knew, looked, looked, loved, loved).

2nd: 88.

Page 292

"It is always wise to look ahead, but difficult to look farther than you can see."

Page 293

21 squares and rectangles.

Page 294

Vert.: rat, pin, dip, vim, tin, peg, nail, wine, glove, disgust, inclined; horiz.: summon, escape, welcome, laughter, curved, pocket, servant, pretend, inverted, violent, suffer. Suffer.

Page 295

22, 55, 77, 198, 264, 275, 286, 506, 539.

Page 296

```
        7    4
   10 8 11  1 30
    8 9     3 20
      24    8
    1          33
      15   17
  1 4 8     3 5 21
      9    50
     32    70
```

Page 297

1st: 4 (the numerical value of the first letter ÷ 2: W = 23 ÷ 2,
      T = 20 ÷ 2, V = 22 ÷ 2, H = 8 ÷ 2).

2nd: dog, bone: dogs love bones
      dog, dodge: the letters of the first are all in the second
      dog, tail: dogs have tails
      dog, tail: as verbs, they are synonyms
      bounce, bone: the letters of the second are all in the first
      escape, dodge: they are synonyms
      escape, cap: the letters of the second are all in the first.

Page 298

Two circles would intersect a triangle, two triangles would
be within a square, three squares would intersect a circle.

Page 299

All the lightface numbers are multiples of 7. The 49 on
the fifth line, second column.

Page 300

1st: E.g., 2 + 1 + 6 + 3 + 7 + 4 + 5 = 28.
2nd: E.g., coat, socks, turtleneck, corduroys, smock, tuxedo,
      cummerbund.

Page 301

1st: $(7 + 6 - 1) \times 2 \div 8 = 3$.

2nd: dissemble, withhold, shelter, screen, obscure, cache, hide, secrete, occult, veil, dissimulate.

Page 302

$2 + 4 + 6 + 8 + 10 + 11 + 13 + 17 + 19 + 21 + 9$
$+ 2 + 3 + 4 + 9 + 2 + 10 + 11 + 12 + 7 + 5 + 1 +$
$2 + 2 + 21 + 23 + 25 + 27 + 3 + 2 + 7 + 1 + 1 =$
300.

Page 303

1st:

16	24	13	7	3
17	4	6	21	18
11	1	23	5	20
22	10	9	14	12
2	25	19	15	8

2nd: pirogue (the only one without a sail).

Page 304

1st: E.g., donkey, monkey, keyed, keyboard, keyhole, hockey, pokey.

2nd: 2, 3, 5, 7, 11 (prime numbers)

5 (+ 2) 7 (+ 2) 9 (+ 2) 11 (+ 2) 13

11 (+ 2) 13 (+ 2) 15 (+ 2) 17 (+ 2) 19

7, 11, 13, 17, 19 (prime numbers from 7 to 19).

Page 305

1st: $5391 + 6804 = 12195$.

2nd: *damp*: pedal, prime, games, cards.

Page 306

1st: E.g., 27 is the only cube; 144 is the only square, the only even number, the only multiple of 12; 235 is the only multiple of 5; 63 is the only multiple of 7; 117 is the only multiple of 13.

2nd: Monotony.

Page 307

"If people behaved in the way nations do, they would all be put in straightjackets."

Page 308

The dominoes progress by 2s (1, 3, 5, 7, 9, 11). The missing domino has a value of 1 (dot pattern 1:0).

Page 309

He is tall, has black eyes, and is wearing a raincoat, not a hat.

Page 310

"I'll meet the raging of the skies, but not an angry father."

Page 311

E.g.: Rose is the only one that is also a color, the only one with thorns, the only climbing plant; iris is the only one that grows from a bulb, the only one that grows in or near water; magnolia is the only evergreen; azalea is the only one with both the first and last letters of the alphabet.

Page 312

48 squares and rectangles.

Page 313

1st: 1 (− 2, + 3, − 4, + 5, − 6).

2nd: E.g., par, part, art, tic, pat, pate, ate.

Page 314

1st: I slew him with the hoe.
      I taught him to hoe.
      Come to the door.
      There come no more to the door.
      No, I slew him there.
      I taught with him.
      No hoe slew him.

2nd: Biwa, Michigan, Huron, Hula, No, Dao, Como, Mead, Leman, Chad, Erie, Eyre. Leman is missing.

Page 315

1st:

2nd: The B on the second line, third column and the A on the fourth line, fifth column should be reversed (the pattern is that each line has a symmetric arrangement).

Page 316

VENICE.

Page 317

1st: E.g., 113, 61, 60, 71, 40, 23, 46, 41, 122.
2nd: hour, shove, review, wavelet.

Page 318

1st: $11 - 7 + 3 = 7$; $8 + 4 - 5 = 7$; $9 + 3 + 3 = 15$;
      $11 - 8 + 9 = 12$; $7 + 4 - 3 = 8$; $3 + 5 - 3 = 5$.
2nd: The product of the first four prime numbers is . . . 30.

Page 319

"There is a superstition in avoiding superstition."

Page 320

1st: 16.

2nd: fools (a, a, all, amongst, and, at, but, but, by, come, dice, fool).

Page 321

1st: 1 (1^2) 9 (3^2) 25 (5^2) 49 (7^2) 81 (9^2)
       2 (+ 3) 5 (+ 4) 9 (+ 5) 14 (+ 6) 20
       1 (+ 6) 7 (+ 7) 14 (+ 8) 22 (+ 9) 31
       19 (+ 6) 25 (+ 6) 31 (+ 6) 37 (+ 6) 43.

2nd: 121, 81: both are squares
     121, 44: both are multiples of 11
     121, 212: both are composed of the same digits
     44, 212: both are even numbers
     44, 212: both are multiples of 4
     27, 81: 81 is a multiple of 27
     163, 347: both are prime numbers.

Page 322

   1, 4, 25, 49, 64, 100, 169, 196, 324, 400.

Page 323

```
        7    9
    4  1  7  8  20
   10  4     6  20
      12    23
    1          36
      17    18
  8  5  4     3  5  25
       1    47
      22    68
```

Solutions

Page 324

1st: band, age: they form the word *bandage*
band, stage: bands play on stage
band, strap: they are synonyms
band, instrument: bands play instruments
age, stage: they rhyme
age, agent: the letters of the first are all in the second
agent, instrument: they are synonyms.

2nd: 8 (the number of letters of each drink x 2).

Page 325

Vert.: sensation, lion, toil, piano, audio, radio, emotion, ionic; horiz.: ovation, fiction, caption, action, scion, pain, main, coin, mission, version, tension, cushion, nib, skin, ionic.

Page 326

Alternate a gray crab with a white crab, the gray crabs getting paler each time. One valid sequence is 7, 5, 9, 4, 3, 2, 6, 1, 8.

Page 327

Two circles would intersect a triangle, zero squares would be within a circle, zero triangles would enclose a square.

Page 328

"I was so long writing my review that I never got around to reading the book."

Page 329

1st: $1 - 2 + 3 - 4 + 5 + (6 \times 7) + 8 + 9 = 62$.

2nd: E.g., Lisbon, Dakar, Boston, Madrid, Tokyo, Canberra, Oslo, Tampa, London, Rabat, Lome, Austin.

Page 330

1st: mollify, conciliate, appease, calm, assuage, satisfy, soothe, pacify, humor.

2nd: $[9 + 8 - (2 \times 7)] \div 3 = 1$.

Solutions

Page 331

64 squares and rectangles.

Page 332

1st: titian (not a shade of blue).

2nd:

8	16	25	4	12
20	3	7	11	24
21	9	13	17	5
2	15	19	23	6
14	22	1	10	18

Page 333

"She was a machine-gun riddling her hostess with sympathy."

Page 334

1st: *byre*: rusty, yearn, beard, robin.
2nd: 7930 + 4526 = 12456.

Page 335

1 + 2 + 3 +5 + 5 + 6 + 7 + 7 + 2 + 5 + 5 + 9 + 5 + 5 + 2 + 4 + 7 + 5 +2 + 6 + 5 + 2 + 3 + 2 + 4 + 1 = 110.

Page 336

Edward's daughter is Helen; his house is Florence.
Francis's daughter is Elisa; his house is Helen.
George's daughter is Gabby; his house is Elisa.
Harry's daughter is Isabella; his house is Gabby.
Isaac's daughter is Florence; his house is Isabella.

Solutions

Page 337

1st: 1 (+ 4) 5 (+ 4) 9 (+ 4) 13 (+ 4) 17
4 (+ 9) 13 (+ 9) 22 (+ 9) 31 (+ 9) 40
1 (+ 7) 8 (+ 7) 15 (+ 7) 22 (+ 7) 29
3, 11, 17, 29, 41 (prime numbers that, when added to another prime number, total 100: e.g., 3 + 97 = 100).

2nd: E.g., vacation, indicate, catalogue, scathing, cathedral, cater, scat.

Page 338

E.g., Orange is the only citrus fruit, the only one which can be peeled without a knife; blueberry is the only one whose seeds you eat, the only berry; melon is the only one that grows on a vine; pineapple is the only word that contains one of the others (apple), melon is the only word that is an anagram for another fruit (lemon).

Page 339

1st: Great.

2nd: E.g., 13 is the only prime number; 22 is the only multiple of 11, the only even number; 9 is the only square, the only multiple of 3; 35 is the only multiple of 5; 119 is the only multiple of 17.

Page 340

1st: 5 (+ 2, − 3, + 4, − 5, + 6).

2nd: E.g., dip, diploma, mat, tic, call, ally, all.

Page 341

The domino values are the first six prime numbers (1, 2, 3, 5, 7, 11). The missing domino has a value of 3 (dot pattern 0:3 or 1:2).

Solutions

Page 342

1st: You hold one and grab the other one with your foot. You nail one to the wall. You set one of them swinging then grab the other. You lengthen one with a piece of string. You climb onto a step ladder. You call someone to help you. You swing on one of the ropes.

2nd: 9 (+ 7) 16 (+ 5) 21 (+ 3) 24 (+ 1) 25
0 (0^2) 4 (2^2) 16 (4^2) 36 (6^2) 64 (8^2)
3 (x 4) 12 (+ 4) 16 (x 4) 64 (+ 4) 68
3 (x 3) 9 (+ 3) 12 (x 3) 36 (+ 3) 39.

Page 343

1st: even (a, against, and, as, at, be, can, despise, despise, dig, eminent, entirely).

2nd: 56.

Page 344

1st: The P on the second line, second column and the R on the fourth line second column should be reversed (the pattern is each upper-right to lower-left diagonal consists of one repeated letter).

2nd:

Page 345

1st: Raven, eagle, flamingo, finch, owl, sparrow, goose, crane, heron. Stork is missing.

2nd: Her husband is that big man.
She got a big fish, her husband a poor one.
That man is her poor husband.
Her husband is poor, but he can fish.
This man can get her a fish.
This man is the one that can get the nearest to her.
Her husband reasons "I can get away."

Page 346

```
        4    7
    7 2 4 7 20
    8 4    6 18
      10   20
    5           35
      24   6
  20 3 5    2 1 31
       1   35
      30   43
```

Page 347

BOOK.

Page 348

27 squares and rectangles.

Page 349

26, 39, 52, 91, 117, 143, 182, 312, 611.

Page 350

1st: give, going, rodent, costume.
2nd: E.g., 19, 53, 36, 47, 106, 69, 88, 63, 76, 49.

Page 351

The crabs in sequence are each missing a different leg or claw starting at the right front leg, then the left, then the right middle, then the left... One valid sequence is 2, 9, 6, 8, 5, 3, 1, 4, 7.

Page 352

1st: E.g., 7 + 2 + 4 + 5 + 1 + 8 + 3 = 30.
2nd: E.g., raven, kestrel, lark, eagle, crane, egret, canary.

Page 353

The lightface numbers are multiples of 3 or 7, but not of both. The 48 on the fifth line, second column.

Page 354

One circle would intersect a triangle, five squares would be within a triangle, four squares would intersect a circle.

Page 355

1st: Two plus eight plus four plus nine minus ten equals . . . 13.
2nd: $2 + 5 + 7 = 14$; $9 - 5 + 2 = 6$; $8 + 3 - 7 = 4$;
$2 + 9 - 8 = 3$; $5 + 5 - 3 = 7$; $7 - 2 + 7 = 4$.

Page 356

"The golden rule is that there are no golden rules."

Page 357

Bernard's son.

Page 358

"His thoughts, few that they were, lay silent in the privacy of his head."

Page 359

1st: E.g., lark, pigeon, hawk, dove, ibis, cuckoo, swan, duck, parrot, finch, owl, raven.
2nd: $1 + 2 + 3 + 4 + 5 - 6 + 7 + 8 + 9 = 33$.

Page 360

1st: $2358 + 9448 = 11806$.
2nd: *maze*: amber, zones, azure, claim.

Solutions

Page 361

Vert.: who, chowder, watchful, childish, uncowled, charming, fetching, why, chime; horiz.: witch, wield, which, stitch, conch, touch, wither, weight, eschew, clothe, cry, chime. Chime.

Page 362

"Society is based on the assumption that everyone is alike and no one is alive."

Page 363

The crabs in sequence have their front claws turned in, then right, then out, then left, then in... One valid sequence is 7, 9, 1, 4, 3, 6, 2, 5, 8.

Page 364

E.g.: Blouse is the only one only worn by women; coat is the only one only worn for cooler weather; socks are the only footwear, the only one worn in pairs; hat is the only head wear, the only 3-letter word; belt is the only one that serves to secure another piece of clothing.

Page 365

52 squares and rectangles.